Interventions in Dementia Care

M. Powell Lawton was Director of Research at the Philadelphia Geriatric Center for 30 years and is now Senior Research Scientist. He is also Adjunct Professor of Human Development at the Pennsylvania State University and Professor of Psychiatry, Temple University School of Medicine. His doctorate was in clinical psychology from Teachers College, Columbia University. He is Editor-in-Chief of the Annual Review of Gerontology and Geriatrics.

Robert L. Rubinstein is Professor of Anthropology at the University of Maryland Baltimore. He is also Senior Research Anthropologist and former Director of Research at the Polisher Research Institute of the Philadelphia Geriatric Center. He has conducted research in the United States and in Vanuatu (southwest Pacific). His research interests include death and dying, the culture of long-term care, and social relations and home environments of older people.

Interventions in Dementia Care

Toward Improving Quality of Life

M. Powell Lawton, PhD
Robert L. Rubinstein, PhD
Editors

 Springer Publishing Company

Springer Publishing Company, Inc.
536 Broadway
New York, NY 10012-3955

Acquisitions Editor: Helvi Gold
Production Editor: Helen Song
Cover design by James Scotto-Lavino

00 01 02 03 04 / 5 4 3 2 1

Library of Congress Cataloging-in-Publication Data

Interventions in dementia care : toward improving quality of life /
    M. Powell Lawton and Robert L. Rubinstein, editors.
        p.   cm.
    Includes bibliographical references and index.
    ISBN 0-8261-1325-7 (hardcover)
    1. Dementia.   2. Quality of life.   I. Lawton, M. Powell
(Mortimer Powell), 1923-   II. Rubinstein, Robert L.
    [DNLM: 1. Dementia—therapy—Aged.   2. Dementia—
psychology—Aged.   3. Quality of Life—Aged.   WT 155 I615
2000]
    RC521 .I586 2000
    616.8'3—dc21   99-059273
                                                                              CIP

This volume is dedicated to the late Dr. Shimon Bergman of Jerusalem, Israel, a Renaissance man who led gerontologists across the world to link research and practice.

Contents

Contributors[1]

Mary Rose Atlas, M.S.W.
Philadelphia Geriatric Center
Philadelphia, PA

Jiska Cohen-Mansfield, Ph.D.
Hebrew Home of Greater Washington
Rockville, MD

Jill Etter, R.N., B.S.N.
Philadelphia Geriatric Center
Philadelphia, PA

Deborah Frazer, Ph.D.
Philadelphia Geriatric Center
Philadelphia, PA

Christine Hallahan, B.A., C.T.R.S.
Philadelphia Geriatric Center
Philadelphia, PA

Karl Kosloski, Ph.D.
University of Nebraska
Omaha, NE

M. Powell Lawton, Ph.D.
Philadelphia Geriatric Center
Philadelphia, PA

Rhonda K. Montgomery, Ph.D.
University of Kansas
Lawrence, KS

Ruth Mooney, R.N., Ph.D.
Philadelphia Geriatric Center
Philadelphia, PA

Marcia G. Ory, Ph.D., M.P.H.
National Institute on Aging
Bethesda, MD

Margaret Perkinson, Ph.D.
Philadelphia Geriatric Center
Philadelphia, PA

Deborah Powell, CNA
Philadelphia Geriatric Center
Philadelphia, PA

Peter V. Rabins, M.D., M.P.H.
Johns Hopkins University
Baltimore, MD

Robert L. Rubinstein, Ph.D.
Philadelphia Geriatric Center
Philadelphia, PA

---

[1]Affiliation at the time the papers were presented.

Holly Ruckdeschel, Ph.D.
Philadelphia Geriatric Center
Philadelphia, PA

Carol Bowlby Sifton
Consultant in Occupational
  Therapy and Dementia Care
Halifax, Nova Scotia
Canada

Kimberly Van Haitsma, Ph.D.
Philadelphia Geriatric Center
Philadelphia, PA

Tracy Wills, B.S.R.D.
Philadelphia Geriatric Center
Philadelphia, PA

Acknowledgments

Edward N. Polisher, Philadelphia Geriatric Center board member and major supporter of the Edward and Esther Polisher Research Institute, was the motivating force for a series of conferences designed to bring researchers and those involved in delivering services to older people together. The chapters in this book were all derived from material presented at a conference on Alzheimer's disease sponsored by Philadelphia Geriatric Center and held in April 1996. Frank Podietz, President, and Robert Silver, Chairman of the Board, gave unlimited support. The conference could not have taken place without the tireless work of the Communications Department and Shelley F. Benedict, Director, and Kimberly Wagman, Assistant Director. Significant financial support for some of the research on which various contributions are based was given by the Harry Stern Family and Joseph Abramson Family Alzheimer's Research Program, the National Institute on Aging, and the Alzheimer's Association. Finally, thanks for manuscript preparation are due Evelyn Gechman.

Introduction

M. Powell Lawton and Robert L. Rubinstein

The cloud of treatment nihilism that has surrounded care for people with dementia shows signs of clearing. For most of this century, the biological origin of Alzheimer's disease and related disorders has traditionally been cited as the reason for making "humane care" the limit of any goal for the care of such people. From the back wards of mental hospitals to the hidden areas of the nursing home of the late twentieth century, the idea of "treatment" for dementia has been considered irrelevant. Even today, limitations on public expenditures for mental health services are based on the idea that psychotherapy should not be done with those whose primary diagnosis is one of the irreversible dementing illnesses. Further, nursing home reimbursement is very likely to be reduced for care given to the demented who do not have major deficits in the activities of daily living.

Because such evidence of the health care system's judgment that dementia is untreatable persists at the turn of the century, is there really any indication that the tide may be turning? We suggest, first, that the reader be alerted to read this book's epilogue by Marcia Ory of the National Institute on Aging to see how this pace-setting federal research agency has undertaken to turn the tide of nihilism. Beyond this effort, however, widespread interest in testing the limits of interventive effort is discernible in activity throughout the long-term-care community. Such interest is apparent in the activities on behalf of community programs for people with dementia and their caregivers under direction of the Alzheimer's Association. Day care and respite care are turning toward the development of expertise and targeted programs for the cognitively impaired. The special problems associated with this type of impairment in providing end-of-life care and support to families with such members has been recognized by several funding agencies.

We see this volume as one of the elements that can contribute to the task of determining where interventive effort is best directed.

An essential complementary task is to set limits on what is believed to be achievable. For a condition whose biological substratum is irreversible, it is tempting to foster unrealistic hope that is good for neither science nor families with an impaired person. The first task of our volume, thus, is to maintain a stance in which empirical science and direct, critical, clinical observation constitute the bases on which hope is allocated.

A second task is to provide a basis for the allocation of hope, one that specifies criteria for recognizing the hopeful signs. We see hope for favorable outcomes of intervention in the domains of functional competence, behavioral symptoms, positive behaviors, and subjective quality of life.

FUNCTIONAL COMPETENCE

We suggest that improvement in performance or maintenance of the ability to perform the tasks of daily living is a positive and universal goal for people with dementing diseases and one that is amenable to change and new learning across a substantial range of cognitive impairment. One of the deficits of much long-term care, whether given in the home or in institutions, is the removal of incentives for independent behavior and the reinforcement of dependent behavior. It is often easier for staff to dress, feed, and wash clients rather than motivate them to do or assist in those tasks themselves. Convincing evidence appears in the literature that incremental progress can be made in keeping these skills alive, at least in mildly to moderately impaired people.

"DISTURBING BEHAVIOR"

This term is politically incorrect today; that is, one can often discern that some behaviors are disturbing to caregivers and onlookers but purposeful and nondisturbing to the person with dementia. Let these facts be accepted. Nonetheless, there is such a thing as a norm for acceptable public behavior. Some behavioral symptoms disturb other care receivers as well as caregivers. Further, even if a behavioral symptom is understandable, what produces the symptoms is often disturbing to the person who exhibits the symptom. Thus, as long as alertness to the many possible origins of such symptoms is maintained by the professional, targeting symptoms for intervention seems quite appropriate. Behavioral symptoms are also among the most amenable to intervention.

POSITIVE BEHAVIORS

Just as "disturbing" behaviors are seen as foci for interventions, there is an oppositely valenced class of behaviors. Positive behaviors are frequently ignored in the care of people with dementia. Behaviors such as basic social interaction, participation in either planned or unplanned activities, or even simple attentiveness while observing other people's behavior are overshadowed as treatment goals by the actually less frequent disturbing behaviors more typically selected as targets for treatment. We see such externally engaging activities as an essential aspect of quality of life.

SUBJECTIVE QUALITY OF LIFE

Much of the literature on the psychopathology of later life depersonalizes individuals with dementia, portraying them as if they had no past history and no current personality. Among such thoughtlessly ascribed losses are the ability to indulge likes and avoid dislikes. Over and above any direct neurological intrusion on the ability to react to or express positive and negative emotional states, there is ample evidence of the continued ability of people with dementia to respond emotionally to the world around them. Subjective quality of life is the balance of positive and negative affects. Such a concept will be demonstrated to be highly relevant to dementing illness (chapter 5).

These four domains represent aspects of quality of life that the physical and social care milieu can enhance or diminish, whether the context be the home, day care, specialized housing, or nursing home. The possibilities for favorable change in functional ability, behavioral adjustment, positive behaviors, and subjective quality of life have been consistently underestimated. We suggest that proper recognition of their potential as care targets will result not only in improved programming but also in the increased motivation of all caregivers, since they will be able to see the positive result of their efforts. It is our hope that the chapters to follow will lead both professional care providers and family members to an appreciation of the concept of incremental change as a tenable treatment goal.

A TAKEOFF POINT FOR DISCUSSING INTERVENTION

The opening chapter by Peter Rabins provides a picture of a novel process for bringing scientific information into the treatment of dementia. Treatment guidelines are meant to distill and make accessible to the maximum number of practitioners current knowledge about a particular illness. Late though its recognition may have come, it is reassuring to see Alzheimer's dementia included among what is available to practitioners. Dr. Rabins' summary lays out the process by which scientific knowledge was sifted, assessed, and converted into treatment-relevant recommendations. Such a process searches for evidence supporting a hope for improvement while simultaneously judging the weight and direction of evidence. Like all efforts to bridge the gap between research and practice, the guidelines as formulated also have their limitations. Evidence continues to accumulate, and the conclusions of 1997 may not be the same as those that would be drawn in 2000. One example might be the impressive amount of research since 1997 attesting to the ability of nonpharmacological behavioral methods to change behavioral symptoms. Nonetheless, this chapter sets the style, with the conclusion that some manifestations of dementing illness were agreed, by an impressive medical consensus, to be treatable.

THE FOUR BASIC DOMAINS FOR INTERVENTION

The next four chapters deal roughly with the domains noted as prime candidates for intervention: functional competence, behavioral symptoms, positive behaviors, and subjective quality of life. In the first of these chapters, Carol Bowlby Sifton discusses active care in an inclusive manner. She illustrates well the interrelatedness of quality among all four domains. Although she treats care directed toward the activities of daily living (ADL) and positive behaviors in great detail, she also shows how attention to these treatment goals is related to the amelioration of behavioral symptoms and how all of these domains are, in turn, reflected in the feelings and attitudes of the care receiver. She assumes the continuity of personality and individual preferences over the course of dementia. A major message from her chapter is that the caregiver will both do a better job and feel better about caregiving if he or she is empowered by knowledge of the elasticity of some manifestations of dementia in the face of informed interventive effort.

In chapter 3, Jiska Cohen-Mansfield deals specifically with the class of behaviors called agitation or "disruptive." She states clearly that "disruptive" is a construction of the observer and discusses further some differences between adaptive and nonadaptive behavioral symptoms. As the creator of the Cohen-Mansfield Cognition Inventory, she presents an authoritative picture of the varieties of disturbed behavior and their measurement. Every clinician will benefit from her review of research that helps define the antecedents and consequences of agitation. Particularly useful is her discussion of the ecology of disturbed behavior, which contains very usable information on how the care environment may be arranged to control agitation. A systematic program entitled *Treatment Routes for Exploring Agitation* is described. This approach is tailored to apply individually to the three major types of agitation: verbal disruptive behaviors, physically nonaggressive behaviors, and physically aggressive behaviors. This chapter makes clear that positive behaviors may forestall the experience of agitation and that disturbed behavior should be probed in terms of its subjective meaning and relevance to quality of life.

Unlike ADL training or behavioral approaches to ameliorating agitation, there is no body of research to assess the results of psychotherapy with the cognitively impaired, to say nothing of any attempts to contrast the efficacy of differing therapeutic approaches. Given this lack, Deborah Frazer provides what is arguably the definitive review of issues pertinent to the use of psychotherapy with dementia patients. Many clinicians encounter such clients without having had much professional training in the dementing illnesses of later life. Therefore the first section consists of a concise introduction to the basic aspects of the major illness categories. The bulk of her chapter reviews methods that have been used by her and others in an effort to tailor therapy to people with dementia. Dynamic, interpersonal, cognitive-behavioral, and other less well known approaches are discussed. Although all of these approaches are in the stage of having simply been used and described by individual clinicians rather than formally validated, Frazer discusses each type of therapy within the framework of what is known about such matters as cognitive function, memory, affect, and other psychological functions that may change with dementia. This chapter deals with both the external behaviors and the interior of the person with dementia and thus speaks to all four of the domains.

The fourth domain, subjective quality of life in dementia, had received little recognition until the past couple of years, reflecting, no doubt, the stereotype that demented people have no inner life. Chapter 5, by Lawton, Van Haitsma, and Perkinson, on affect in dementia may be thought of as a prelude to interventions that may be applied to any of the four domains. Their point is that one way in which cognitively impaired people speak about their feelings, care, and desires and aversions is through the nonverbal language of their emotions. These authors' research attesting to the validity of direct judgments of affect state in dementia is reviewed. The major purpose of the chapter, however, is to instruct raters in the use of their Apparent Affect Rating Scale. They suggest that direct-care staff and family caregivers may learn to be more effective in serving all the domains of quality if they are attuned to the care receiver's signals of satisfaction or dissatisfaction with care. Such sensitization enables them to recognize that people with dementia have an inner life and that these subjective states continue to vary meaningfully with positive and negative behaviors and contexts. They argue that the caregiver's sense of efficacy may be strengthened by having the expertise to "read" when his or her efforts are successful.

COMPLEX INTERVENTION SYSTEMS

The final two substantive chapters share the feature of designing interventions that operate far beyond the one-to-one therapist-to-patient model. In the first instance, an entire intervention team is involved; in the other, caregiving as a system involving care receiver, primary caregiver, other informal caregivers, and formal caregiving individuals and organizations.

Chapter 6 by Kimberly Van Haitsma and her collaborators illustrates well a cycle of knowledge production whose structure is noteworthy as a model. A specific research endeavor at the authors' institution (part of the collaborative study described by Ory in chapter 8) tested an intervention package in traditional experimental fashion. One facet of the intervention package was a new way of structuring the care planning process. As only one component of that process, planning was impossible to single out. However, it had a certain type of validation in its appeal to staff and exportability to other locales. Therefore a more extensive report on that experience is provided by Van Haitsma et al. The next step in knowledge production would be another randomized trial to test the impact of the care planning model. The application of the model begins with a structure that characterizes the components and temporal sequence of an ideal model. Essential aspects of a team include interdisciplinary representation, rotation of meeting leadership, recording, information feedback, and a process that focuses upon the remediable aspects of the person's behavior and subjective state. The process is analyzed by means of an illustrative history as well as consideration of barriers to success and problem-solving approaches to deal with the barriers. Like the chapter on psychotherapy, this chapter offers a plethora of ideas for clinical exploration in pre-evaluative fashion.

Although we rarely think of it in such terms, by far the most prevalent intervention directed toward dementia is the attentions given by informal caregivers. We judged it to be very important to acknowledge this source of care amid the other professionalized types of intervention. Unlike some of the systematically conceived interventions, caregiving is infinitely varied: there is no package to serve as a model, everyone does it differently. In fact, this is the theme of the chapter by Rhonda Montgomery and Karl Kosloski, that there is great diversity but also a pattern common to much caregiving. An understanding of this pattern will be useful to researchers, professional care providers, and informal caregivers themselves. After an extremely useful review of state-of-the-art knowledge regarding who provides care, the core of the chapter offers a highly original analysis of caregiving as a career. "Markers" (clearly identified as varying in presence and timing and across families) are described as ways of organizing some of the many influences on the form of caregiving in any individual case. Roughly chronological markers include performing caregiving tasks, self-definition as a caregiver, performing personal care tasks, seeking formal services, consideration of a nursing home, institutionalization, and termination of the caregiving role. In the last section of the chapter, the uses of this view of the caregiving career and its dynamics are discussed in ways that are relevant to people in every helping profession. Although their emphasis is on the caregiver more than on the person with dementia, the caregiver may be seen as a mediating influence on the care receiver, whereby favorable effects of stress reduction and positive supports on the caregiver exert an important indirect effect on the person with dementia.

AFTERWORD

In the final chapter, Marcia Ory indicates how some of the issues of treating dementia and supporting caregivers have been investigated by focused initiatives of the National Institution on Aging. These initiatives have had an impact beyond the specifics of their findings (many of which are still emerging) in making researchers and service-delivery professionals think about difficult questions. Going beyond clinical care itself, her chapter provides a fitting larger structure for conceptualizing how targeted intervention fits into the context of caregiving and dementia as a whole.

As a whole, this collection approaches the topic of interventions for dementia as a scientific endeavor that should be based on relevant research. Each intervention has its theoretical substructure, which is used liberally to point to clinically useful suggestions in the many instances where data are still lacking. One can imagine each chapter being followed in another few years with reconsideration of the theories and clinical suggestions advanced in this book in light of new data, some of it hopefully stimulated by thoughts from this volume.

1

The Development of Treatment Guidelines for Alzheimer's Disease

Peter V. Rabins

In the past, treatment planning was solely an issue between the patient and practitioner. In recent years, however, more than 1800 formal treatment guidelines (for more than 500 clinical conditions) have been developed by the medical profession for the purpose of identifying effective therapies and standardizing clinical care. This trend heralds dramatic changes in clinical practice and in medical scholarship (Anderson, 1994). This chapter uses the development of treatment guidelines for Alzheimer's disease as an example of this phenomenon. It briefly reviews the process that led to the development of the treatment guideline process in general—a specific process used to devise treatment guidelines for Alzheimer disease—and reviews the major content of the guidelines themselves.

WHY DEVELOP GUIDELINES NOW?

Several reasons can be cited for the dramatic surge in the number of treatment guidelines. First, research over the past decade and a half has demonstrated that clinical practice varies widely by geographic area in the United States and among practitioners in the same field working in the same geographic area but that it differs between specialists and nonspecialist practitioners. Furthermore, most studies have found that these differences in care result in no discernible benefit for patients. The wide variance in the cost of different procedures, the lack of differences in outcomes, and the lack of standardized approaches have all fueled an effort to distill the published literature and determine which treatments are clinically effective and which are cost-effective.

A second impetus for the development of treatment guidelines has been the increasing percentage of gross domestic product (GDP) applied to health care. In the United States, 15% of GDP is related to health expenditure, a figure 50% higher than that of western European countries. No studies have demonstrated that this higher "investment" has resulted in public health benefit. For example, using gross statistics such as life expectancy, no clear benefit can be shown for the greater investment in health in the United States. The rapid rise in health care costs has been used as evidence that heath care is inefficient and has led to the suggestion that significant cost savings would result if health care expenditures were limited to those procedures which could be shown to be cost-effective.

A third and less discussed basis for treatment guidelines is the explosion of knowledge that has occurred in the past 40 years. Prior to World War II, there were few effective medical or psychological therapies for dementing diseases. A concerted research effort over the past half century has resulted in the development of a wide range of effective treatments for individuals and populations. This explosion of knowledge has been difficult to keep up with and it is thought that some of the variation in practice might be due to lack of knowledge among practitioners.

PROCESSES FOR DEVELOPMENT TREATMENT GUIDELINES

The desire for more standardized approaches to treatment has led to the development of several processes for identifying the most efficient and effective practices for consolidating knowledge about them and making recommendations for their widespread adoption.

One process for guideline development resulted from the formation of the Agency for Health Care Policy and Research (AHCPR), a federal government agency that forms panels to develop guidelines and funds grants to perform outcome studies and so provides information from which specific guidelines can be developed (Maklan, Greene, & Cummings, 1994). The agency invites knowledgeable experts on various aspects of a disorder to participate in a panel, which hears verbal "testimony" from a variety of invited experts and performs a metanalysis (Hasselbad & McCrory, 1995) of the existing published literature. Each panel is supported by a staff whose job it is to help develop standards for reviewing articles, help panel members review those articles, and perform statistical analyses to determine efficacy (benefits in small trials of selected individuals) and effectiveness (benefits in representative population samples) of available treatments. The AHCPR has published a number of documents that disseminate its findings. These include articles in major journals likely to be read by clinicians treating the condition in question, pamphlets for the public, and in-depth documents reviewing the methods and data.

A second approach to guideline development relies on surveys of self-reported practice. Respondents are usually individuals identified as "experts." Because these treatment guidelines are based on expert opinion rather than reviews of existing literature, this approach has the strength that it reflects practice in "the real world" as opposed to the atypical characteristics of subjects in typical randomized controlled trials. This is an advantage because practice sometimes outpaces the published literature and often must address issues that are not considered in randomized clinical trails—for example, the treatment of individuals with multiple disorders and those on several medications. Clinical practice sometimes incorporates new uses for treatments that have been developed for other purposes and are often not studied by the product developers or manufacturers. A major drawback of this approach is that it is not based on primary data collected to determine efficacy. Equally problematic is the suspicion that clinicians often do things out of habit or with a "herd mentality" and utilize therapies found to be ineffective when appropriate studies are performed.

A third approach is to convene a panel of recognized experts and have them perform a metanalysis of published studies and current practice. This approach was used by the American Psychiatric Association (APA) to develop a guideline for the treatment of persons with Alzheimer's disease and other dementias. The panel's analysis is sent out in several iterations to experts and organizations with an interest in the disorder and made available to other practitioners. All comments are then reviewed, addressed, and incorporated into the guidelines when supported by data.

A fourth approach is to compare treatments naturalistically, that is, to determine the outcomes of treatment across different practitioners or settings (Ware et al., 1996). This method utilizes the different practice patterns that have emerged naturally as the basis for assessing effectiveness. Its major disadvantage is that bias affects how treatments are chosen for any individual patient.

These four approaches are less desirable substitutes for the more ideal route into treatment guidelines that devolves from randomized clinical trials (RCT). These are experimental trials in which research subjects are randomized to an active treatment or a placebo control group. In this ideal form, ratings of specified a priori outcomes are carried out by raters who are unaware of the treatment status of the subjects and in which the subjects themselves are unaware of whether they have received the active or placebo treatment.

DEVELOPMENT OF TREATMENT GUIDELINES FOR DEMENTIA

This section describes a specific process by which a set of treatment guidelines for dementia was developed. An initial review of the published literature on dementia suggested that relying only on RCTs would not be possible. Most challenging was the fact that these standards could not be applied to many areas of nonpharmacological treatment of dementia. That is, the RCT methodology had been widely used in studies of pharmacological agents but much less widely applied to the assessment of the efficacy of such forms of treatment as environmental and behavioral therapies. As a result of these limitations of the published literature, the APA panel established two standards. The first was that data for pharmacological studies were required to meet minimum standards of a RCT. The second standard was that recommendations for nonpharmacological treatments could be based on methodologically less rigorous studies such as single-blinded studies, case series, and naturalistic outcome studies. Judgments regarding the quality of the data influenced the strength with which the recommendations were advanced.

Initially the panel members divided up the primary targets of treatment (cognitive symptoms, noncognitive/behavioral symptoms, caregiver distress) and examined pharmacological and nonpharmacological treatments in each area. Each panel member attempted to locate all published studies on his or her assigned topic by first utilizing standard indices such as the *Index Medicus* and *Psychological Abstracts* and then using reference lists, personal knowledge, and other leads to obtain data that could be reviewed. The findings of this review were presented to the panel members. Consensus was then sought on the efficacy of each treatment and on the strength of the data that were used to generate a recommendation.

Three major iterations of the written document were produced. The first draft was reviewed by all participants on the panel and the staff of the APA, who oversee the guideline development process. After revisions, a second draft was mailed to approximately 80 experts in the treatment of dementia. These experts were drawn from a variety of clinical, geographic, and ethnic backgrounds. The comments from this group were reviewed and the guidelines revised. A third mailing was then sent to a large number of organizations and individuals with an interest in dementia. These individuals included psychiatrists and nonpsychiatric physicians, nonphysicians, organizations whose members had an interest in dementia; district branches of the APA; and potentially interested proprietary organizations. All comments that were received were reviewed and each was specifically addressed. Changes in the document were made they when felt to be appropriate and the document was submitted to the APA committee overseeing guideline development. The guideline was published as a supplement of the *American Journal of Psychiatry* (American Psychiatric Association, 1997).

MAJOR FINDINGS OF THE APA GUIDELINE PANEL

Overall, the panel felt there were a number of effective treatments for Alzheimer's disease and noted that pessimism about treatment seemed unwarranted. All findings are referenced in the panel's report but are not referenced here. The panel did not review the data on effectiveness of assessment because its charge was to focus on treatment. Nevertheless, the guideline begins by noting the importance of a thorough assessment and differential diagnosis. Indeed, it notes that a thorough evaluation is necessary for the development of treatment planning. The panel emphasized the importance of considering financial and legal issues and suggested that the clinician recommend to family members that they seek adequate counsel on these issues.

Therapies for Cognitive Impairment

Two effective pharmacological treatments are available for the cognitive disorder caused by Alzheimer's disease. These agents, tacrine (Davis et al., 1992) and donepezil (Rogers et al., 1996), are modestly effective. Donepezil, since it has fewer side effects and more convenient dosing, will likely be the treatment of choice until other pharmacotherapies ar developed. More recently, vitamin E and selegiline have been shown to delay both nursing home placement and functional decline. While it is presumed that their mechanism of action is via antioxidant pathways, there is no direct evidence that this explains their efficacy. Since the course of cognitive decline was not affected by vitamin E, selegiline, or a combination of both agents, their use as a primary therapy is not yet established. Nevertheless, the panel felt the low cost and high safety of vitamin E supported its usage even though there was only one published study.

There is no evidence that nonpharmacological therapies can improve cognitive performance for longer than the training session, and the panel did not recommend their use.

Therapies for Noncognitive Behavioral and Psychiatric Symptoms

Patients with Alzheimer's disease experience high rates of noncognitive/behavioral/psychiatric symptoms. These include hallucinations, delusions, depression, physical aggression, pacing, wandering, and sleep disorder.

A meta-analysis of pharmacotherapy has demonstrated that neuro-leptic antipsychotic drugs are 19% more effective than placebo for the treatment of physical aggression/agitation. In spite of the wide use of these drugs for other symptoms, the panel could not cite data that these agents are effective for the treatment of delusions and hallucinations. The panel noted their widespread use and recom-mended them with low confidence. A variety of other pharmaco-logical agents (anticonvulsants, antidepressants, beta blockers, stimu-lants) have been reported as efficacious in case studies, small case series, and small randomized trials. The panel did not feel that the data supported recommending specific agents for specific symptoms but noted that some of these therapies are likely to be efficacious and made no recommendation against their use. The panel did note that benzodiazepines can have adverse effects on cognition and that data are lacking on their efficacy.

There are insufficient data to support the efficacy of nonpharmaco-logical treatments of noncognitive/behavioral/psychiatric symptoms. Nevertheless, the panel concluded that combining data on a variety of treatments—including music therapy, pet therapy, activity therapy, and regular scheduled activity—did support the conclusion that they are modestly effective. The panel also concluded that these treatments probably operate by a nonspecific shared mechanism and that it is unlikely that any one of them would be more effective than the others.

Treatment of Caregiver Distress

Many studies document high levels of distress in persons providing care to individuals with Alzheimer's disease. Of 11 randomized con-trol trials, 9 demonstrated that nonpharmacological interventions with caregivers were effective in decreasing symptoms of depression and emotional distress. The most effective treatments appear to com-bine education and emotional support. One trial suggested that such interventions may delay nursing home placement.

Other Issues

The panel noted that persons with dementia are treated in a variety of settings and that specific issues may arise in these settings. In the acute medical setting, a supportive environment, frequent orientation, and monitoring for the development of delirium are necessary. In the long-term-care setting, a structured environment that stimulates and supports residents, attention to medical comorbidity, and a knowledgeable staff are important for optimal care. One study demonstrated that nursing home patients randomized to a care condition that emphasized daily activities, careful review of medications, and a discussion of strategies for managing behavior problems required fewer restraints and had fewer behavior problems than patients receiving standard care.

CONCLUSION

Alzheimer's disease and other dementias affect a significant number of older Americans. Pessimism regarding treatment is unwarranted (American Psychiatric Association, 1997). While no treatments are available to cure or arrest Alzheimer's disease and most other dementias, those therapies that are available can improve the quality of life of patients and caregivers.

REFERENCES

American Psychiatric Association (1997). Practice guideline for the treatment of patients with Alzheimer disease and other dementias of late life. *American Journal of Psychiatry, 154* (May Supplement), 1–39.

Anderson, A. (1994). Measuring what works in health care. *Science, 263,* 1080–1082.

Davis, K. L., Thal, L. J., Gamzu, E. R., Davis, C. S., Woolson, R. F., Garcon, S. I., Drachman, D. A., Schneider, L. S., Whitehouse, P. J., Hoover, T. M., Morris, J. C., Kawas, C. H., Knopman, D. S., Earl, N. L., Kumar, V., Doody, R. S., and tacrine collaborative study group (1992). A double-blind, placebo-controlled multicenter study of tacrine for Alzheimer's disease. *New England Journal of Medicine, 327,* 1253–1259.

Hasselbad, V., & McCrory, D. C. (1995). Meta-analytic tools for medical decision making: A practical guide. *Medical Decision Making, 15,* 81–96.

Maklan, C. W., Greene, R., & Cummings, M. A. (1994). Methodological challenges and innovations in patient outcomes research. *Medical Care, 32,* JS13–JS21.

Rogers, S. S., Friedhoff, L. T., and donepezil study group (1996). The efficacy and safety of donepezil inpatients with Alzheimer's disease: Results of a US multicentre, randomized, double-blind, placebo-controlled trial. *Dementia, 7,* 293–303.

Ware, J. E., Bayliss, M. S., Rogers, W. H., Kosinsku, M., & Tarlov, A. R. (1996). Differences in 4-year health outcomes for elderly and poor, chronically ill patients treated in HMO and fee-for-service systems. *Journal of the American Medical Association, 276,* 1039–1047.

2

Maximizing the Functional Abilities of Persons with Alzheimer's Disease and Related Dementias

Carol Bowlby Sifton

Agnes was in the advanced stage of Alzheimer's disease (AD). She could barely speak, but she could move around quite well. In fact, she could move around so well that she seldom sat still. Keeping her safe was a real challenge for her caregivers. Although Agnes could speak only a few words, she spent a great deal of her day moaning, shouting, and calling out. This was another big challenge for her caregivers. And nothing her caregivers tried seemed to relieve Agnes's agitation and distress . . . until a summer student came to visit and thought about ways to enable Agnes to continue her valued life occupation as a homemaker.

Agnes's new caregiver brought some unbreakable dishes, a dishpan, tea towels, and soap and helped her to get started washing dishes. To everyone's amazement, Agnes spent several hours carefully washing, drying, and stacking the same dishes over and over. And even more amazing, during this entire time Agnes didn't call out or begin to pace.

Caregivers continue to help Agnes to get started washing dishes. She continues to be happy and calm while doing the dishes. Agnes has something to do to occupy her, which is meaningful to her. Her quality of life has been enhanced. She is no longer such a challenge to care for. Some of the symptoms of her incurable disease have been treated.

ALZHEIMER'S DISEASE AND RELATED
DEMENTIAS AND ACTIVITY

For Agnes and the millions of other persons with Alzheimer's disease and related dementias (ADRD), supporting the basic human need for involvement in meaningful occupation (functional performance) can effect a very powerful treatment (American Alzheimer's Association, 1995; Bowlby, 1993; Bowlby Sifton, 1998; Cohen & Eisdorfer, 1986; Hellen, 1992; Mace, 1990; OTA, 1987; Reichenback & Kirchman, 1991; Zgola, 1987). *We all need something to do. And most importantly, we all can do something.*

ADRD are neurological diseases with primarily behavioral symptoms (American Psychiatric Association, 1996; OTA, 1987). This is a standard and widely repeated definition. Unfortunately, how this is acted out in day to day life is not so widely understood. Professional and lay caregivers can be so overwhelmed by behavioral changes, like those Agnes was experiencing (e.g., repetitive questioning, wandering, restlessness, apraxia, or disorientation) that they can forget two important facts: these behavioral changes are neurologically based and the person has continuing abilities. Consequently, the focus of care can become so directed toward responding to these challenging or negative behaviors that essential goals of care, such as enhancing the quality of life and enabling maximal functional independence, can be lost. The most important question really is, *"How can we support positive behavior, engagement in meaningful activity?"* and not *"How can we cope with negative or challenging behaviors?"* There is a need to take a leaf from the book of Agnes's inventive caregiver. The intent of this chapter is to provide an overview and some basic guidelines for supporting engagement in meaningful activity (occupation). It is directed toward a broad spectrum of caregivers, informal and formal, including family, paraprofessional health care aides, and a whole range of professionals, such as nurses, social workers, rehabilitation specialists, recreationists, and psychologists, to name a few.

The content is divided into three main sections. The first addresses making use of continuing abilities in day-to-day care. Appreciating that the person with ADRD has persisting strengths and focusing daily activities around these strengths is the foundation of this approach to care. Deficits associated with ADRD have such a profound impact on the ability to carry out activities in the usual way that caregivers often find it difficult to bridge the gap between abilities and activity. In response to this difficulty, the second section turns to some practical guidelines for engaging persons with ADRD in occupation. Problems with memory and other cognitive abilities complicate the rehabilitation process with persons with ADRD. However, it is important to appreciate that this should not and need not exclude the person with ADRD from rehabilitation. The last section addresses this issue as well as some theoretical considerations with regard to rehabilitation and the client with ADRD. Guidelines for facilitating the rehabilitation process are provided.

It is important to clarify the meaning given here to the term *occupation* (activity). *It is, quite simply, everything we do during the course of a day,* and includes the activities of daily living (e.g., brushing teeth, eating lunch, making a phone call), work (e.g., playing with grandchildren, stuffing envelopes) or leisure (e.g., looking out the window, talking to a friend, or weeding the garden). Occupation (activity) is not just something that happens Friday mornings at 10 but includes every aspect of the entire day. *Engagement in occupation is engagement in life itself.* From this perspective, enabling engagement in meaningful occupation is not solely the responsibility of the activity or recreation or occupational therapist but the responsibility of every individual who comes in contact with the person with ADRD (American Alzheimer's Association, 1995; Bowlby, 1993; Bowlby Sifton, 1998; Hellen, 1992; Kitwood & Benson, 1995; Mace, 1990; Zgola, 1987). Every interaction—for example, passing someone in the hall—provides an opportunity for engagement in occupation.

Humans are, by nature, doing people. Notice, that we introduce ourselves to others by saying something about what we do; for example, I am a mother, a gardener, a friend, a therapist, etc. The centrality of doing is so deep in our culture that it is a standard part of formal (How *do* you *do?*), or informal greetings (How are you *doing?*). Lawton describes the powerful human need to do as follows: " . . . empirical evidence overwhelmingly supports the idea that both animals and people will create activity where none exists, as if the void of doing nothing or the same thing for too long was as aversive as having too many demands" (Lawton, 1985, p. 131). Humans are meant to be engaged in occupation, and absence of occupation leads to illness. There is a strong association between meaningful occupation and well-being. And of particular interest here, continued engagement in lifelong occupations is associated with healthy aging (Bonder & Wagner, 1994; Bowlby, 1993; Bowlby Sifton, 1998; Cohen, 1988; Ruuskanen & Ruoppita, 1995). The effect of ADRD on the person's capacity "to do" is staggering. During the long course of the disease, there is hardly a facet of life that is not affected. And yet even in the severely demented, we continue to observe the overwhelming need to do, for the hands to be occupied, what may appear to the outside observer to be totally purposeless activity—ceaselessly patting the rumpled piece of tissue, smoothing and straightening the sweater edge, pacing the same worn path, repeating the same hollow phrase so many times that others may be driven to distraction.

The behaviors speak of the persisting need to do; the desperation to continue activity, to be occupied, even when neurological and physical deficits stand in the way of independent adult occupation. The basic human need to find pleasure and satisfaction in purposeful activity, to exert mastery over the environment, persists. This need is spoken of by Cohen and Eisdorfer (1986) as follows:

> Perhaps the most important concern of many patients is the need to participate as actively as possible for as long as possible [p. 64]. . . . dementia is not a hopeless condition for which nothing can be done. Patients are human beings—first, last and always. They usually live for years with the disease, and those are long and difficult years. The challenge during that time is to maximize an individual's ability to function at the highest possible level [p. 221].

The profound impact of meaningful occupation for the person with ADRD is illustrated by the opening clinical anecdote. It is also supported by clinical experience and research findings of a strong association between the lack of meaningful activity and the presence of depression (Teri & Logsdon, 1991) and the occurrence of challenging behaviors (Rabinovich & Cohen-Mansfield, 1992). Quayhagen and Quayhagen (1989) found that teaching home caregivers to engage the person with ADRD in activity reduced the occurrence of challenging behaviors and improved the cognitive and emotional functioning of the person as well as the self-esteem of the caregiver.

Disease-associated deficits in initiation, planning, problem solving, motor coordination, and other domains make it progressively more difficult for the person with ADRD to organize his or her own occupation. The following sections provide some suggestions on ways to overcome these deficits and enable continued engagement in occupation.

THE CONTINUING ABILITIES OF PERSONS WITH ADRD

Although still far from ideal, the health care system has become much better at diagnosing and describing the symptoms (deficits) associated with ADRD. Unfortunately, this has not necessarily been accompanied by an enhanced understanding of how to promote wellness, of maintaining the continuing abilities of the person with ADRD, and of how these abilities may be used to compensate for deficits. This section provides an overview of eight continuing abilities of persons with ADRD and the ways in which these abilities may be used by all caregivers to enhance functional performance.

The person with ADRD may often have excess disability—that is, disability greater than that caused by the disease itself (Bowlby, 1993; Brody, Kleban, Lawton, & Moss, 1974; Brody, Kleban, Lawton, & Silverman, 1971). In other words, there is a gap between what the person can do (ability) and what the person actually does do (performance). This is known as the *disability gap,* and it has been suggested that interventions to reduce the disability gap represent one of the most important treatment opportunities available for persons with ADRD (Cohen, 1988). *It is essential to appreciate that although there is, at present, no treatment for the disease, there are treatments for the person with ADRD.*

Detailing the many factors leading to excess disability is beyond the scope of this brief chapter. However, making use of continuing abilities is one of the most effective ways to reduce this disability gap and enhance functional performance and hence provide a treatment for the person with ADRD. These continuing abilities have been grouped under eight headings:

- Habitual skills/procedural memory
- Humor
- Emotional memory/emotional awareness
- Sociability/social skills
- Sensory appreciation/sensory awareness
- Motor function

- Musical responsiveness
- Long term memory

Perhaps these can be collectively recalled as the mnemonic **HHESSMML**, suggesting that people with ADRD have more skills than we sometimes give them credit for.

Each of these areas of strength, or continuing ability, is discussed briefly, with some suggestions for how they may be used to enhance quality of life and compensate for deficits. By focusing our attention on these continuing abilities, we are able to compensate for losses, reduce excess disability, and enhance functional performance. For further references and more details in all of these areas see Bowlby, 1993, and Bowlby Sifton, 1998.

Habitual Skills/Procedural Memory

Although memory loss is the hallmark symptom of ADRD, it is important to appreciate that there are several different types of memory. The classic memory loss of ADRD is *episodic* memory. This type of loss is specific to particular events and would involve remembering, for example, what you had for breakfast, who you had Christmas dinner with, or where you went on your twenty-first birthday. As the disease progresses, the ability to recall these events becomes more and more impaired. *Semantic* memory, on the other hand, refers to memory for general knowledge, which is fixed and does not depend on particular events. This would involve remembering what sorts of foods are eaten for breakfast, the date of Christmas, or your birthday. In general, semantic memory is less impaired, since the information is constant and the person can use cues to assist recall. However, as the disease progresses, the gaps in semantic memory become more and more noticeable.

For both of these types of memory, it is important to appreciate that *recognition is much better preserved than recall*. For example, a mother may recognize a daughter but be unable to recall her name. Or a patient may recognize his house but be unable to recall the address. It is important to make use of this continuing ability by responding to nonverbal indicators of recognition, such as a smile. And, most especially, it is crucial not to confront the person with recall deficits, such as the common practice of asking, "Do you know me?" or "What's my name?" Such questions remind people of their deficits—rather than emphasizing their abilities—and set a negative and threatening tone for the conversation. In all interactions with the person with ADRD, it is important to make use of the continuing ability for recognition as well as social skills while at the same time compensating for deficits by providing basic orientation information (e.g., who you are, where you are, the date, etc.). *This information is provided for reassurance,* not for recall, as was the case with the unsuccessful reality orientation approach (Bowlby, 1993).

Procedural memory is remembering "how"; it is the most basic memory system. Procedural memory is triggered by familiar cues associated with the action. Being handed a toothbrush spread with toothpaste triggers the procedural memory for brushing teeth. Offering an arm while familiar music is playing triggers the procedural memory for dancing. Responses based on procedural memory are rather rigid, stereotyped responses, which are not usually adaptable to changes in the environment or method. These are the habitual skills for those actions that adults have repeated countless times in their lives, such as drying the dishes, sweeping the floor, self-feeding or setting the table. Research indicates that persons with ADRD retain procedural memory skills in spite of difficulty with verbal or conscious recall (Dippel & Hutton, 1988). In order to call forth these overlearned or habitual skills it is important that:

- *The cues in the environment be familiar* (e.g., to facilitate procedural memory for self-feeding, the food served, the method of serving, and the eating area should be as close as possible to lifelong experience).
- *The method of carrying out the activity be familiar* (e.g., to encourage the person to have a bath, use the same type of bathing experience. A bath on a bath bench is not the same as a bath directly in the tub).
- *The cues be presented in a subcortical—i.e., not requiring conscious processing—nonverbal manner.* For instance, to encourage the use of procedural memory to put on a sweater, simply hand the person the sweater rather than offering confusing verbal instructions.

Sense of Humor

> When reminded that he had his shoes on the wrong feet, Mr. Bellefountain, eyes twinkling, replied, "There's nary a thing I can do about that, they are the onliest feets I got."

Caregivers have a ready repertoire of the ways, such as the above, in which a lifelong sense of humor is preserved throughout ADRD and bypasses other communication deficits. Like Mr. Bellefountain, the person with ADRD frequently uses humor to cover for memory loss, continues to enjoy amusing family or local anecdotes, and will use mime and jest to tease. These subtle ways to protect adult dignity should be supported, with care, of course, not to be fooled about the person's actual capacity to perform. Humor is a good way to divert the person who is becoming agitated. Gentle humor, laughing with, not at the person, should be encouraged to support a light-hearted and playful care atmosphere for both the person and the caregiver.

In addition, a good laugh is therapeutic, relieving tension and bringing pleasant feelings. Laughter has positive physiological effects on respiration and circulation. It also promotes the release of neuro-transmitters (e.g., catecholamine), which increase alertness and sensations of pleasure and also reduce pain (from endorphins) (Bowlby, 1993).

Emotional Awareness and Emotional Memory

The person with ADRD retains emotional awareness—the capacity to experience the full range of emotions: love, joy, fear, sorrow, anger, frustration, etc. (Bowlby, 1993; Cohen, 1988; Hellen, 1992; Kitwood & Benson, 1995; Mace, 1990; OTA, 1987; Zgola, 1987). The deficit is in the expression of these emotions. By providing nonverbal opportunities for expression of emotion and nurturing, the caregiver greatly enhances quality of life and makes use of this continuing ability in order to compensate for deficits. Experiences such as involvement with pets, plants, and children, listening to music, or engagement in meaningful activity, provide opportunities for emotional expression which bypass verbal communication deficits. It is essential to acknowl-edge the expression of feelings, even if the source cannot be determined. Comments such as "John, you seem sad today, can I help you?" acknowledge and validate the person's feelings and help to overcome stress. The person with ADRD is particularly aware of the emotional state of others and may be extra sensitive to these moods. This heightened sensitivity, perhaps due to dampened rationality, also appears to enhance the spiritual awareness of persons with ADRD. Supporting lifelong spiritual practices takes on special significance (Seicol, 1995).

Emotional memory is the memory of the feeling of the event. All the available evidence suggests that persons with ADRD retain emotional memory. That is, they may not remember the fact of going on the picnic, but they do remember having had a good time. By enhancing the positive emotional memories of activities, we facilitate future participation. This includes required activities, such as bathing, where the positive aspects can be increased by, for example, providing options for control and choice (e.g., asking "Would you like to have your bath now or after breakfast?" and using music, favorite towels, soft robes, or scented powders).

Emotional memory can also be called on to relieve caregiver stress. Caregivers can easily become overwhelmed by the seeming futility of what they do, as the person with ADRD forgets the factual events around caring actions such as a visit, a treat, or an outing. Comments such as "You never talk to me anymore" immediately after a lengthy visit can lead the caregiver to feel defeated. The following anecdote is an illustration of the power of emotional memory.

Alice was in the advanced stage of Alzheimer's disease. She required twenty-four-hour care and assistance with all activities of daily living, which was provided in a nursing home. In spite of these severe deficits, every Sunday Alice went to church with her son and his family and afterwards to their house for Sunday dinner. Usually she sang along and smiled happily during the hymns at church and enjoyed the greetings of other churchgoers. Afterwards, at dinner, she was sometimes able to help set the table or mix the salad. Whatever she was able to do or not do, surrounded by her family, she smiled happily and was free of the restlessness which so often disturbed her at the nursing home. During the Easter church service, Alice didn't smile or hum during the music and had to be fed the communion bread. She dozed through much of the service and during the car ride home and her family decided that Easter dinner would be just too much and drove back to the nursing home. When the car stopped at the entry doors, Alice sat up with a start and opened her eyes wide. In a clear voice she demanded, "What am I doing back here already?" Alice was not able to articulate the factual order of what she did on Sundays, but she had a strong emotional memory of a pleasant family time after church.

This powerful anecdote not only illustrates the persistence of emotional memory but also reminds caregivers that *in spite of failures to verbally recall what we have done, the person with ADRD carries an emotional memory, or a memory in the heart. What we do does make a difference.*

Sociability and Social Skills

Among the several hundred persons with dementia that I have met or worked with, I have yet to encounter one who did not respond in some way to the offer of a handshake. This is but one of the countless overlearned adult social behaviors that persist throughout the course of ADRD (Baum, Edwards, & Morrow-Howell,1993; Reisburg, 1983). The more socially adept the person has been, the more these skills can be relied on. These persisting social skills encompass a whole range of behaviors—often repeated phrases or greetings, such as "lovely weather," "nice dress," "delicious coffee," or greeting and welcoming a guest, being part of a party. By supporting and encouraging sociability in groups and individually, deficits in memory, reasoning, and language can be compensated for. The person may, for instance, no longer be able to prepare lunch for friends, but he or she can still greet the person at the door and serve as host or hostess at the table. This facilitates function and supports self esteem.

Consider the opening example of the handshake. With proper cuing, even persons in the advanced stages respond by shaking a hand held out in greeting. And what a simple way to accomplish so many ends: it supports self-esteem by recognizing the person in an adult, familiar way; through touch the greeter communicates caring; the greeting brings the person to attention and creates the opportunity for eye contact; if the greeter smiles warmly and asks "How are you?" there is more often than not a "Fine, thank you" in return.

The person with ADRD is frequently very skilled at using overlearned or vague social responses to cover up memory loss—e.g., feigning recognition of a visitor. This is an excellent coping mechanism and a way to maintain dignity in social situations. However, caregivers must be cautious not to mistake this behavior for the persistence of higher skills, such as memory and judgment, in vital areas of self-maintenance, such as medication management or nutrition.

Sensory Appreciation/Sensory Awareness

The primary sensory receptive areas of the brain remain largely untouched by the processes of ADRD (Bowlby, 1993; Aronson, 1988). Experiencing the sounds, smells, sights, tastes and movements of everyday life can serve as an ongoing source of pleasure for the person with ADRD. It is through these sensory cues that humans understand and respond to the world around them. *The need for sensoristasis, a particular level of sensory stimulation that is necessary to support normal brain functioning, persists until death.*

Although the sensory receptive areas of the brain are largely undamaged, other deficits associated with ADRD, such as perceptual problems or lowered initiative, render the person susceptible to sensory deprivation. In addition, he or she may be experiencing sensory losses associated with normal aging. These risks are further complicated by living in an unsuitable environment, whether the individual may experience sensory deprivation (e.g., bland colors and textures in the environment) or overstimulation (e.g., intercoms and the coming and going of staff).

Sensory stimulation, the presentation of sensory-rich materials in a manageable and understandable way, enables the person to overcome these obstacles to make use of persisting sensory abilities and to experience the pleasures of life through the senses. In turn, this stimulation is a cue for an active, or functional, response. Structured sensory stimulation is a skilled clinical intervention, with research-based evidence supporting effectiveness (Bowlby, 1993; Hames-Hahn & Llorens, 1989; Lawton, Van Haitsma, & Klapper, 1994; Reichenback & Kirchman, 1991). This is a very simplified account of what is really a very complex topic; a detailed discussion is beyond the scope of this chapter. *However, by using some of the basic sensory stimulation techniques, every caregiver can enhance both the pleasure and functional responses of persons with ADRD, particularly in the middle and advanced stages.* These techniques have been found to be particularly effective in enabling self-feeding.

In order to make use of the senses for stimulation, it is important to:

1.   Use sensory-rich, familiar, everyday objects (for example, fresh flowers or an orange).
2.   Focus on only one sense at a time (for example, the smell of the flowers or the feel of the orange skin).
3.   Draw the person's attention to the item (for example, by placing the flowers under the person's nose or gently placing his or her hands on the stems or on the orange).
4.   Encourage the person to make an adult, functional response (for example, putting the flowers in a vase or peeling and eating the orange).

Everyday activities provide thousands of opportunities for sensory stimulation. Using steps 2, 3, and 4 above, caregivers can enable the person to be more responsive and involved in life as well as providing pleasurable sensory experiences.

Primary Motor Function

Although there are some exceptional cases where the person may experience apraxia and other motor symptoms early on, *primary motor function is largely unaffected by the processes of ADRD until the later stages* (Aronson, 1988; Bowlby, 1993; Zgola, 1987). This is a tremendous resource for active treatment. The importance of exercise and movement in promoting improved physical health—for example, for the cardiorespiratory system—is well established, even with frail nursing home residents. In addition, there is growing evidence that movement enhances mental alertness in everyone, including with persons with ADRD. Movement is a basic human need; at a fundamental level, we humans are meant to move. We can all identify with this if we think about how fatigued we feel after sitting for several hours while attending a meeting or a conference. People with ADRD who pace or "fidget" with their hands are acknowledging this same need to move.

As the disease progresses, the person with ADRD has increasing difficulty with coordinated movement. These difficulties progress from distal (e.g., leg movement) to central (e.g., trunk musculature to maintain an upright posture) and from fine (e.g., coordinated use of the fingers) to gross (e.g., coordination of the legs for walking). As these problems increase, the importance of supporting continued movement and maintaining a normal seating posture becomes even greater. Through this support, later stage complications of contractures, aspiration pneumonia, and skin breakdown can be minimized.

In the early and middle stages, the major impediment to movement is difficulty with getting started. Caregivers can compensate by encouraging familiar, functional activities that include movement (e.g., dancing, sweeping the floor, raking leaves, going for a walk). Music is also an important aid in initiating movement. A safe and stimulating indoor or outdoor walking or wandering route should be provided. It is safety, not the pacing, that is the concern, as persons with ADRD who pace have been found to be physically healthier than those who do not. Structured exercise programs can be helpful in the early and middle stages. Following a routine that uses functional activities and demonstration is helpful in facilitating participation.

Responsiveness to Music

The area of the brain that responds to and appreciates music, generally the right hemisphere, is among the most frequently preserved response systems. The continuing ability to respond to and appreciate music opens the door to many possibilities. Music has an amazing capacity to speak, to enliven and enrich, and to bypass the many communication deficits of ADRD. In doing so, it brings pleasure, not only from the music itself but also by taking the person back to the rich emotional associations with favorite and familiar music.

Everyone has probably witnessed the person with ADRD who is able to sing the words to a familiar song and yet is primarily nonverbal. By providing opportunities to respond in this way, an alternate form of communication is encouraged and self-esteem is supported. So although music therapy is a skilled intervention carried out by trained professionals, every caregiver can access some of the benefits of music by providing such simple opportunities as humming a favorite tune.

On the other hand, it is important to appreciate that music in and of itself does not produce some kind of magic effect. A full guide to the use of music with persons with ADRD is beyond the scope of this chapter. A few essential guidelines are mentioned, however. First of all, it is important to make a connection between the person and the music in order to compensate for difficulties with taking initiative. Some techniques include starting to sing along, gently taking person's hands and swaying or clapping to the music, helping to start tapping along with the rhythm with hands or feet, or taking an arm to encourage familiar dance steps. It is also important to pay careful attention to music selection. Not all music appeals to all people. Consult with significant others to learn about favorite types of music and cherished songs. In general, music from the era when the person was in his or her midteens to midtwenties is the best recalled.

Bearing these considerations in mind, music can be used to support quality of life and function in several ways. Above all, offering familiar music provides an opportunity to experience pleasure. Calming, familiar music at bedtime can promote sleep. Engaging the person in humming or singing along with a favorite song can be a good distracter to reduce distress—for example, during bathing. A comforting and reassuring environment that includes music can be a help in coping with wandering and sundowning (Whitcomb, 1993, 1994). Music serves as a stimulus to movement.

Long-Term Memory

Although more and more cuing is required as the disease progresses, for the person with ADRD, long-term memories remain much more intact than recent memories (Bowlby, 1993; Haight, 1991). The person may not remember what happened 5 minutes ago or 5 years ago, but try 50 years ago. Those memories that are best preserved involve what might be called "mountaintop lifetime experiences," such as the first day of school, winning the championship, getting married, first job, first car, etc. Assisting the person to recall these experiences brings pleasure and supports self-esteem by taking the person back not only to the experiences themselves but also to the associated feelings. This is of particular importance as the person with ADRD, like all aging persons, works through the developmental task of summing up and putting life experiences in perspective. Verbalization and involvement in activity (e.g., by helping to prepare the batter for a specialty cake) are encouraged.

The use of reminiscence in these ways is an important tool during all interactions with persons with ADRD. This should not be confused with what is known as "life-review therapy," which is a skilled intervention, conducted by a trained professional to work through unresolved past issues. Reminiscence, as referred to here, is a simple or storytelling reminiscence for the purpose of bringing pleasure in recalling past life experiences. Reminiscence groups have been found to be very successful in meeting the goals described above.

In using reminiscence on a daily basis, some guidelines are of particular importance. Opinion-seeking questions, rather than questions with right or wrong answers, should be used. Use questions such as "What is your favorite . . . ?" "What do you like best about . . . ?" "Does this look familiar to you?" In this way, the person with ADRD can succeed, since everyone can offer an opinion, but some may not succeed if asked "What is this called?" Provide hands-on cues, such as old kitchen utensils, vintage clothing, or other artifacts that the person can touch and feel, thus compensating for difficulties with verbal understanding. It is important to know the person's life story in order to use cues to assist in recalling life experiences. A wonderful tool for family and paid caregivers is a small hand-held photo album containing labeled pictures of important people and events, over the course of the person's life. This provides an almost instantly successful opportunity for reminiscence and activity, which most seem never to tire of. Finally, it is important to appreciate that the purpose of using reminiscence is not to encourage the person to live in the past. Having recalled the past experiences, help the person to come forward in time by making comparisons to the present. For example, if the conversation has been about the person's first wristwatch, a connection could be made to the present by looking at your own watch and talking about how much watches cost now.

GUIDELINES TO ENGAGING PERSONS IN OCCUPATIONS

While people with ADRD have many continuing abilities, they also have numerous deficits, which make it increasingly difficult for them to continue with independent adult activity in the usual way. However, as discussed at the outset, the need to do persists. As skill loss progresses over the course of ADRD, caregivers often find it challenging to support continued functional activity. This section provides some general guidelines that can help caregivers bridge the gap between the need to do and diminishing skills for independent activity.

As discussed at the outset, engagement in occupation is an essential human need. *However, it is important to appreciate that it is the process of engagement in occupation that is central, not the product or outcome.* The focus throughout should be on the person and his or her responses and needs, not on the activity itself. *For the person with ADRD, the present moment is the most important moment,* the future cannot be anticipated, and yesterday is forgotten or dimly recalled. The goal of engagement in occupation is to enhance, enliven, and enrich this present moment. While using the following guidelines, pay careful attention to such factors as physical comfort, whether the activity provides the appropriate level of challenge to enable success, whether the person understands what is happening, and—above all—if the person is experiencing pleasure (Bowlby Sifton, 1998; Feldt & Ryden, 1992).

- *Make use of continuing abilities,* HHESSMML, as outlined in the previous section.
- *Support the continuation of a familiar lifestyle and facilitate the use of procedural memory by structuring daily routines around lifelong habits, values, and roles.* This becomes particularly important when the person requires long-term care. *The Personal Care Book,* available from the Alzheimer Society of Canada offices, is an excellent tool to gather this information from family members and significant others, and provides a tremendous asset in enabling other caregivers to be consistent throughout the continuum of care (Alzheimer Canada National Office, 1320 Yonge Street, Suite 201, Toronto, Ontario, Canada, M4T 1X2. Tel: 416-925-3552).
- *Help to initiate the activity.* Decreased initiative is one of the most debilitating symptoms of ADRD with regard to engagement in activity. Unfortunately, this is often mistaken for a lack of interest. However, if the caregiver acts as a "starter" for familiar activities, the person can often continue on his or her own. Some examples would be using hand-over-hand guidance to start self-feeding;

gently taking the arm to start walking; setting up work activities such as folding laundry, peeling vegetables or stuffing envelopes.

- *Provide the appropriate level of cuing.* Adult behavior relies almost exclusively on verbal cues, such as "Here is your lunch" to initiate activity. It is a standard assumption that if people do not respond to this cue by starting to eat, they are unable to feed themselves and need to be fed. However, they may simply need other types of cues—*nonverbal, demonstration or physical guidance*—in order to begin eating.

  When putting on a shirt, the cues might look like this: "Here's your shirt to put on" (*verbal cue*). Touch the person's hand and point to the shirt (*nonverbal cue*). Start to put on the shirt yourself (*demonstration*). Start to gently guide the person's hand into the sleeve (*physical guidance*). It is often necessary to use a combination of these cues.

- *Break the task into manageable steps (task analysis), providing cues for each step as needed.* Simple daily tasks, such as brushing teeth, are usually thought of as one activity. In fact, almost all activities are made up of many steps or sequences of steps. Depending on the level of detail used, brushing teeth (e.g., taking the top off the toothpaste, picking up the toothbrush, etc.) actually consists of anywhere from 12 to 35 steps! The person with ADRD often forgets the sequence of these steps; in a sense, each step becomes another task, and cuing is needed for each separate step.

- *Begin at a step where the person can succeed.* No caregiver could possibly have the time or patience to guide the person with ADRD through each and every activity of the day, one step at a time. However, the person can still participate if some of the steps are done in advance and the person begins at a point in the sequence where he or she can succeed. With the previous example of brushing the teeth, the person could be handed the toothbrush with the paste already on it. If unable to do the entire activity of preparing a cup of tea or coffee, the person can still be guided to stir in the milk and sugar. If the person is unable to follow a recipe and measure, he or she can still stir the liquid into the dry ingredients for muffins.

- *Try backward chaining.* Backward chaining means (re)learning the last step of the activity first and then working backwards until each step is mastered. So, for example, with eating, the last step is bringing the spoon loaded with food to the mouth. The caregiver can help to initiate this step with hand-over-hand guidance until procedural memory takes over. The next step to work on would then be loading the spoon with food.

- *Adapt the task and/or the environment.* There are any number of ways to change either the materials used (e.g., finger foods when utensils can no longer be managed) or the method (e.g., a sponge bath instead of a tub bath) to enable success (American Alzheimer's Association, 1995; Bowlby, 1993; Bowlby Sifton, 1998; Hellen, 1992; Zgola, 1987). Changes to the environment, such as a hand rail or a wall-mounted carpet strip leading to the bathroom, are effective ways to promote function and safety (Bowlby Sifton, 1998; Calkins, 1988; Cohen & Wiseman, 1993; Coons, 1991; Olsen, Ehrenkrantz, & Hutchings, 1993). At the same time, it is important to introduce these changes with sensitivity to personal routines and habits as well as to avoid introducing too many changes at once. An occupational therapist can assist in assessing and developing customized environmental and task adaptations. These are vital but enormous issues, which are only mentioned here.

- *Provide manageable choice/opportunities for personal control.* Independent adults make literally dozens of choices every day, from what to have for breakfast to whether to change jobs. As ADRD progresses, the ability to use judgment and reasoning to make choices becomes more and more impaired. However, the need to exercise control and adult autonomy persists. It is important to appreciate that having opportunities for control is not the same thing as being independent. Caregivers can enable autonomy by reducing the number of choices to a manageable level. In this way, every activity can provide an opportunity for making choices and feeling in control. Ask, for instance, if the person would like to wear the red shirt or the green shirt; eat a ham sandwich or a tuna sandwich; take a bath now or after breakfast. These choices are in contrast to the usually unsuccessful general questions, such as, "What would you like to wear (or eat) today?" Overwhelmed by the enormousness of the choices in such a question, the person with ADRD will usually find it safer to say nothing. During daily routines, finding simple ways to enable participation supports the sense of self; for example, passing the wet towels for the laundry; choosing a cookie from the plate rather than being given one; holding a facecloth during bathing.

- *Organize equipment/materials in advance.* Supporting the person with ADRD in engagement in occupation requires all of our attention. By having everything thought out and prepared in advance, full attention can be given to this process and the flow of the sequence of the steps is not disrupted.This is particularly important during complex activities such as bathing.

- *Use communication techniques that anticipate a positive response.* One of the key approaches for promoting engagement in occupation is to invite participation in a non-threatening manner but one that assumes that the person is going to participate. It is crucial that this be balanced with the assurance that you will be there to assist and with the understanding that, if he or she is distressed, the person has the right to refuse. Some examples of this approach are gently taking the person's arm to begin walking while saying "I have lunch all ready for us; I need your help to stir some cookie dough" (or fold the laundry or weed the garden or . . .) or "I would like you to come and have a cup of tea with me." In this way the person is assured that you will be there to help, but at the same time there is a noncoercive expectation of participation. On the other hand, if the person is approached in the standard way (e.g., "Would you like to go for a walk?") he or she may be unsure of what is expected and uncertain of success; therefore the answer will usually be no.

- *Explain all procedures, every time, to compensate for memory loss.*

- *Ensure privacy and limit distractions.* The person with ADRD has progressive difficulty with maintaining attention and filtering out irrelevant stimuli. Even common daily distractions such as the hum of the refrigerator or the noise of traffic coming through an open window can distract him or her from the task at hand. More obvious distracters—such as other conversations, radios, and televisions—can be absolutely overwhelming and prevent the person from being able to attend to a meal or the conversation. Relatively simple interventions, such as turning off the radio or providing a screen in the common room to reduce visual distraction, can have a profound effect.

- *Allow plenty of time.* For the person with ADRD, every step of the sequence requires more time for processing and responding.

Be prepared to allow as much time as possible, remembering the importance of focusing on the person and the process of occupation, not the product.

- *Ensure consistency in routines and approaches.* The person with ADRD is primarily an association learner, which means that any changes to the steps, materials or environment may appear to be a whole new task (Neistadt, 1996). In order to promote success, it is essential that routine daily activities be done in the same way, using the same steps and directions every time. More details on the implications for the rehabilitation process are found below.

Facilitating the Rehabilitation Process with Persons with ADRD

This section examines some theoretical considerations with respect to the rehabilitation process and the client with ADRD, provides a few examples of successful rehabilitation studies, and offers guidelines for engaging the person with ADRD in the rehabilitation process. There is growing evidence that the role of occupation in the treatment and care of persons with ADRD is critical. In fact, *engagement in occupation or activity-focused care is becoming the model of care for persons with dementia.* This is described by Kitwood (1995) as the "*new culture of dementia care,*" replacing the medical model of care, which has not been adequate to meet either the needs of the person with ADRD or her or his caregivers.

For the rehabilitation specialist, this presents both an exciting opportunity and a challenge. We have the opportunity to offer our expertise to enhance the quality of life for millions of persons with ADRD and their caregivers. On the other hand, we are challenged not only to adapt the rehabilitation process to match the skills of the person with ADRD but also to examine our practice and drop those last vestiges of the medical model. We are challenged to think not only about the what and how of what we are doing, but also the why.

Mr. Tolliver was in the middle stage of Alzheimer's disease and was admitted to a large, urban acute care hospital for management of chronic obstructive pulmonary disease. He was a cheerful, easygoing gentleman who had been managing to stay in his lifelong rural home with the support of his wife. Although he was rather perplexed by all of the activities of the hospital, he remained, for the most part, cooperative with hospital routines. In fact, he rather got to like the "room service and attention" provided by the nursing staff. The team became concerned that he would lose both physical and mental capacity should this continue. Enter the occupational therapist, who began an ADL retraining program, which included morning bathing and dressing. Mr. Tolliver maintained his cheerful disposition, but when he was encouraged to wash his genitals he replied, "I never knew it was so important to be washing down there all the time, but they make a big deal about it around here."

This anecdote provides an illustration of several important considerations of the "why" of the rehabilitation process. While there is no doubt that maintenance of self-care skills, especially in an acute care setting, is very important, we must also be very sure to stand in the shoes of the client and consider whether this focus is in keeping with his or her lifelong values and habits; is this a "big deal" for this client? Is this occupation any more meaningful than supporting other leisure or work occupations? Would he rather have a cup of tea or look at family pictures? Would he experience more success and satisfaction from these occupations? There is tremendous emphasis on ADL occupations in home care, acute care, and rehabilitation settings. As rehabilitation specialists, we need to learn from this gentleman and ask ourselves whether being able to wash himself is a "big deal" for this client; whether we have considered work and leisure occupations in our assessment and intervention plan; whether we have educated family and other caregivers in ways to support continued involvement in lifelong personal routines as well as about engagement in the whole realm of occupational performance.

In contrast, as one progresses through the continuum of care to long-term care, these considerations need to be reversed. In this setting, the emphasis on occupation has traditionally taken a 180-degree shift away from ADL to leisure occupations. Here, individualized restructuring of care around the continuation of lifelong personal routines has transformed the functional performance of the residents. Jo Anne Rader creatively describes new staff roles as those of the "magician, the carpenter, the detective and the jester" (Rader, 1995, p. 20). *Whatever the terms used, the restructuring of care has vastly improved the quality of life of residents, empowered front-line staff, improved job satisfaction, and all but eliminated the use of restraints. At the same time, it does not increase care costs and may even reduce them* (American Alzheimer's Association, 1995; Bowlby, 1993; Greene Burger, Fraser,

Hunt, & Frank, 1996; Happ, Williams, Strumpf, & Burger, 1996; Hellen, 1992; Hoffman & Kaplan, 1995; Jones, 1996; Rader, 1995).

At all stages on the continuum, the rehabilitation specialist is challenged to consider the "why" and maintain a balance in self-care, leisure, and work occupation which is in keeping with client values and needs. Theressa Perrin wisely expresses this as follows: "What is surely of overwhelming importance is comfort, contentment, well-being. Making better is still the central objective, but it is making feel better, rather than making do better" (Perrin, 1995, p. 67).

With these considerations in mind, there is a role for the rehabilitation of persons with ADRD, especially in the earlier stages when learning is less difficult. Research in this area is just beginning, and there are some promising outcomes on the effect of specific retraining with persons in the early stages of ADRD. For example, repeated training with environmental support resulted in improved performance and reduced cueing with some simple instrumental ADL (IADL) tasks (e.g., setting the table or getting a soft drink) (Josephsson et al., 1995); daily training in ADL/IADL tasks (e.g., washing hands and face, dressing, writing) demonstrated a significant improvement in performance, with a carry-over effect to untrained activities (Zanetti et al., 1993); structured practice in the gross motor activity of ball tossing demonstrated a posttraining carryover (Dick et al., 1996) and cognitive stimulation activities resulted in improved MMSE scores (Breuil, Detrotrou, & Forette, 1994). These interventions were very time-intensive, and there was no investigation of the ways in which these skills may have been transferred to the home setting or affected the care needs at home. Nonetheless, they are a hopeful demonstration that persons with ADRD can learn and indicate some of the conditions under which they learn best. The reader is referred to the work of Neistadt (1996) for more information on using the information processing model to enhance the learning of the older adult.

The following guidelines, in combination with an understanding of communication techniques, are suggested for ADL retraining and other rehabilitation approaches with this population.

- *Plan rehabilitation goals collaboratively with the caregiver.* The person with ADRD is dependent on the caregiver to support rehabilitation gains in occupational performance. The caregiver is in effect the case manager and the professional the case consultant (Bourgeois et al., 1996; Bowlby Sifton, 1998). If the goals and intervention plan are not shared by the caregiver, there is little likelihood that they will be maintained.

- *Learning should be failure-free.* Since the person with ADRD is primarily an association learner, these learning experiences should be as free of errors as possible, as the person usually cannot solve problems and generalize from these errors but will simply learn the incorrect way to do something.
- *Emphasize procedural memory learning*—i.e., remembering how to do things.
- *Incorporate motor components.* Incorporating movement in the learning—for example, the response to repeated questions—makes use of a continuing ability and reinforces the learning through a more accessible modality. For example, write the answers to often repeated questions such as "When do I go to the day program?" and post them in a prominent place. Every time the person asks the question, walk with her or him to read the answers. Persons with ADRD will probably never learn not to ask the questions, but with the use of motor activity, they may learn to walk to answer the questions.
- *Train repeatedly, using exactly the same cues and sequences of steps.* The person with ADRD learns at a basic level, and any variations in the task will be perceived as a new task. Consistency is absolutely essential. For both the professional and family caregiver, it may be necessary to write out the steps and verbal cues to avoid changes.
- *Training should be done in the actual environment.* The person with ADRD has difficulty generalizing learning from one setting to another, and even small changes in the environment can make one task seem like another, different one. So, although ADL retraining in acute care or rehabilitation settings is important in terms of maintaining and encouraging occupational performance in general, there should be no expectation that this learning will be transferred to the home setting, particularly as the disease progresses. It is often a better use of professional time to set up a home training program with the home caregiver.
- *Multiple repetitions, without long gaps between sessions, should be used.*
- *Use one-step commands.*

- *Collaborative goal setting is especially important.* Due to problems with initiative and insight associated with the disease, the person with ADRD needs frequent reminding about the goals and purposes of the training.
- *Use ample positive feedback.* This is always an important part of rehabilitation, but for persons with ADRD and their fragile self-esteem, it is vital.

John Angus was a retired farmer and greenhouse operator who was living in a special care unit. He continued his lifelong love of working with plants but found little opportunity to follow through on this activity, as his severe apraxia and coordination difficulties made it almost impossible to do any of these activities independently. John Angus was the perfect participant for a garden club that the occupational therapist was developing. On his first visit, as his hands were guided to the potting soil, he broke into joyous laughter and leaned back with a sigh of contentment saying "Ahh, this is just heaven, and I had no idea that heaven was so handy to home."

Enabled once again to have his hands working with soil and plants, to be engaged in a lifelong meaningful occupation, John Angus was content, untroubled by his usual bursts of distress and agitation. His self-esteem flourished.

CONCLUSION

The information in this chapter has provided the reader with a basic introduction to the ways in which such a transformation of functional abilities can be facilitated for every individual with ADRD. We began with an overview of the essential role of engagement in meaningful occupation, including functional activities, in the treatment and care of persons with ADRD. The following sections provided guidelines for various ways in which engagement in occupation can be enabled. Through making use of continuing abilities, such as emotional awareness or procedural memory, caregivers can reduce excess disability and facilitate function. The guidelines for enabling engagement in activity offer ways in which caregivers can bridge the gap between the loss in skill that accompanies ADRD and the need to be involved in meaningful occupation. The last section addresses issues of particular concern to rehabilitation specialists working with persons with ADRD, from both a theoretical and a practical perspective. Guidelines for supporting the rehabilitation process with persons with ADRD are provided.

REFERENCES

American Alzheimer's Association (1995). *Activity programming for persons with dementia: A source book.* Chicago: Author.

American Psychiatric Association (1994). *Diagnostic and statistical manual of mental disorders,* 4th ed. (DSM-IV). Washington, DC: American Psychiatric Association.

Aronson, M. (Ed.). (1988). *Understanding Alzheimer's disease.* New York: Charles Scribner's Sons.

Baum, C., Edwards, D., & Morrow-Howell, N. (1993). Identification and measurement of productive behaviours in senile dementia of the Alzheimer type. *The Gerontologist, 33,* 403–408.

Bonder, B., & Wagner, M. (1994). *Functional performance in older adults.* Philadelphia: F. A. Davis Company.

Bourgeois, M., Schulz, R., & Burgio, L. (1996). Interventions for caregivers of patients with Alzheimer's disease: A review and analysis of content, process, and outcomes. *International Journal of Aging and Human Development, 43,* 35–92.

Bowlby, C. (1993). *Therapeutic activities with persons disabled by Alzheimer's disease and related disorders.* Gaithersburg, MD.: Aspen Publishers, Inc.

Bowlby Sifton, C. (1998). *At home with dementia: A resource manual for professionals working in the home with persons with Alzheimer's disease and related dementias.* Ottawa, ON: Canadian Association of Occupational Therapists.

Breuil, V., Detrotrou, J., & Forette, F. (1994). Cognitive stimulation of patients with dementia: Preliminary results. *International Journal of Geriatric Psychiatry, 9,* 211–217.

Brody, E., Kleban, M., Lawton, M., & Moss, M. (1974). A longitudinal look at excess disabilities in the mentally impaired aged. *Journal of Gerontology, 29,* 79–84.

Brody, E., Kleban, M., Lawton, M., & Silverman, H. (1971). Excess disabilities of mentally impaired aged. *The Gerontologist, 11,* 124–132.

Calkins, M. (1988). *Design for dementia: Planning environments for the elderly and the confused.* Owings Mills, MD: National Health Publishing.

Cohen, D., & Eisdorfer, C. (1986). *The loss of self.* New York: W. W. Norton.

Cohen, G. (1988). *The brain in human aging.* New York: Springer.

Cohen-Mansfield, J., & Marx, M. (1990). The relationship between sleep disturbances and agitation in a nursing home. *Journal of Aging and Health, 2,* 42–56.

Cohen, U., & Weisman, G. (1993) *Holding onto home.* Baltimore, MD.: The Johns Hopkins University Press.

Coons, D. (Ed.). (1991). *Specialized dementia care units.* Baltimore: Johns Hopkins University Press.

Dick, M., Shankle, R., Beth, R., Dick-Muehlke, C., Cotman, C., & Kean, M. (1996). Acquisition and long term retention of gross motor skill in Alzheimer's disease patients under constant and varied practice conditions. *Journal of Gerontology: Psychological Sciences, 51,* P103–P111.

Dippel, R., & Hutton, J. (Eds.). (1988). *Caring for the Alzheimer patient.* Buffalo: Prometheus Books.

Feldt, K., & Ryden, M. (1992). Aggressive behavior: Educating nursing assistants. *Journal of Gerontological Nursing, 18,* 3–12.

Greene Burger, S., Fraser, V., Hunt, S., & Frank, B. (1996). *Nursing homes: Getting good care there.* San Luis Obispo, CA: American Source Books.

Haight, B. (1991). Reminiscing: The state of the art as a basis for practice. *International Journal of Aging and Human Development, 33,* 1–32.

Hames-Hahn, C., & Llorens, L. (1989). Impact of a multi-sensory occupational therapy program on components of self-feeding behavior in the elderly. In E. Taira (Ed.), *Promoting quality long term care for older persons.* New York: Haworth Press.

Happ, M., Williams, C., Strumpf, N., & Burger, S. (1996). Individualized care for frail elders: Theory and practice. *Journal of Gerontological Nursing, 22,* 6–14.

Hellen, C. (1992). *Alzheimer's disease: Activity-focused care.* Stoneham, MA: Butterworth-Heinemann.

Hoffman, S., & Kaplan, M. (1995). *Special care programs for people with dementia.* Baltimore, MD: Health Professionals Press.

Jones, M. (1996). *Gentle care: Changing the experience of Alzheimer's disease in a positive way.* Burnaby Lake, BC: Moyra Jones Resources.

Josephsson, S., Backman, L., Borell, L., Nygard, L., & Bernspang, B. (1995). Effectiveness of an intervention to improve occupational performance in dementia. *The Occupational Therapy Journal of Research, 15,* 36–49.

Kitwood, T., & Benson, S. (Eds.). (1995). *The new culture of dementia care.* Bradford, UK: Hawker Publications.

Lawton, M. P., Van Haitsma, K., & Klapper, J. (1994). A balanced stimulation and retreat program for a special care dementia unit. *Alzheimer Disease and Associated Disorders, 8,* 133–138.

Lawton, M. P. (1985). Activities and leisure. In *Annual Review of Gerontology and Geriatrics,* Vol. 5. New York: Springer.

Mace, N. (Ed.). (1990). *Dementia care: Patient, family and community.* Baltimore: Johns Hopkins University Press.

Neistadt, M. (1996). An information processing approach to functional skills training with older adults. *Physical and Occupational Therapies in Geriatrics, 14,* 19–38.

OTA (Office of Technology Assessment). U.S. Congress (1987). *Losing a million minds: confronting the tragedy of Alzheimer's disease and other dementias.* OTA—BA-323 Washington, DC: U.S. Government Printing Office.

Olsen, R., Ehrenkrantz, E., & Hutchings, B. (1993). *Homes that help:Advice from caregivers for creating a supportive environment.* Newark, NJ: New Jersey Institute of Technology Press.

Perrin, T. (1995). A new pattern of life: Re-assessing the role of occupation and activities. In T. Kitwood & S. Benson (Eds.), *The new culture of dementia care.* Bradford, UK: Hawker Publications.

Quayhagen, M. P., & Quayhagen, M. (1989). Differential effects of family-based strategies on Alzheimer's disease. *The Gerontologist, 29,* 150–155.

Rabinovich, B., & Cohen-Mansfield, J. (1992). The impact of participation in structured recreational activities on the agitated behavior of nursing residents: An observational study. *Activities, Adaptation & Aging, 16,* 89–98.

Rader, J. (1995). *Individualized dementia care: Creative, compassionate approaches.* New York: Springer.

Reichenback, V., & Kirchman, M. (1991). Effects of a multi-strategy program upon elderly with organic brain syndrome. *Physical and Occupational Therapy in Geriatrics, 9,* 131–151.

Reisburg, B. (Ed.). (1983). *Alzheimer's disease: The standard reference.* New York: The Free Press.

Ruuskanen, J., & Ruoppila, I. (1995). Physical activity and psychological well-being among people aged 65 to 84 years. *Age and Aging, 24,* 292–296.

Seicol, S. (1995). Creating spiritual connectedness for persons with dementia, a Plenary presentation at the American Alzheimer's Association annual conference, Chicago, IL.

Teri, L., & Logsdon, R. (1991). Identifying pleasant activities for Alzheimer's patients: The Pleasant Events Schedule-AD. *The Gerontologist, 31,* 124–127.

Whitcomb, J. (1993). The way to go home. *The American Journal of Alzheimer's Care and Related Disorders & Research, 8,* 1–10.

Whitcomb, J. (1994). "I would weave a song for you": Therapeutic music and milieu for dementia residents. *Activities, Adaptation & Aging, 18,* 57–74.

Zanetti, O., Frisoni, G., De Leo, D., Buono, M., Bianchetti, A., & Trabucchi, M. (1995). Reality orientation therapy in Alzheimer disease: Useful or not? A controlled study. *Alzheimer's Disease and Associated Disorders, 9,* 132–138.

Zgola, Z. (1987). *Doing things.* Baltimore, MD: Johns Hopkins University Press.

3

Approaches to the Management of Disruptive Behaviors

Jiska Cohen-Mansfield

Disruptive behaviors include inappropriate verbal, vocal, or motor activity that does not result from the obvious needs or confusion of the agitated individual. The inappropriate nature of agitated behavior is judged from the perspective of an observer rather than that of the agitated person; the observer's viewpoint may be subjective. Deciphering the meaning of agitation requires continuous effort.

Disruptive behaviors can be described as the following syndromes: aggressive behaviors, physically nonaggressive behaviors, and verbally agitated behaviors. Based on several studies, different meanings seem to correspond to different disruptive behaviors. Most of these behaviors are likely to be associated with discomfort, which may include physical pain, physical restraint, and feelings of depression or loneliness. In contrast, some of the behaviors, especially in the physically nonaggressive category, may be adaptive and not an indication of discomfort. Other disruptive behaviors may result directly from neurological damage.

Several approaches were used to treat these behaviors, based on the interpretation of the reasons for the disruptive behavior. A model of intervention strategies with the different types of disruptive behaviors is described. The challenge of further refining and individualizing these approaches is also discussed.

Disruptive behaviors are a major obstacle in the care of a person suffering from dementia. They bring challenges to caregivers both in the home and in the nursing home. Frequently, it is because family members are not able to cope with these disruptive behaviors at home that they are then forced to institutionalize their relative. In the nursing home, higher staff-to-resident ratios are often required in order to control agitated behaviors of residents.

Disruptive or agitated behaviors have been defined as *inappropriate verbal, vocal, or motoric activity that is not judged by an outside observer to result directly from the needs or confusion of the agitated individual* (Cohen-Mansfield & Billig, 1986).

These comprise a variety of inappropriate behaviors, including repetitive acts, such as repeating the same word continuously; behaviors that deviate from social norms, such as opening one's blouse in public; and aggressive behaviors directed toward oneself or others. Although not disruptive, inappropriate behaviors that may not disturb anyone, such as repetitive mannerisms, should not be overlooked, because they may provide information about the inner state of the person who is suffering from dementia.

It is the caregiver who characterizes any behavior as disruptive. Often, the labeled disruptive behavior may be caused by an older person's physical need, such as fatigue or the need to go to the bathroom, and this need not being obvious to the caregiver. Indeed, the older person suffering from dementia may not even be consciously aware of such needs and thus may not be able to report them even when their verbal skills are intact. On the other hand, behaviors that are clearly a result of a need, such as an accident on the way to the bathroom, or behaviors that obviously result directly from the cognitive impairment suffered by the individual, such as getting lost on the way to the dining room, are not included in this category of disruptive behaviors.

The research on which much of what follows is based was conducted in a large suburban nursing home. Two major projects were undertaken. In the first, nurses, social workers, physicians, and family members provided information concerning the psychosocial, medical, and behavioral status of the residents as well as about the residents' premorbid life. This study is summarized in Cohen-Mansfield and colleagues (1992). The second project involved a detailed systematic observation of 24 very agitated, cognitively impaired residents in the same institution over a 3-month period and is summarized in Cohen-Mansfield and Werner (1995). Additional research done by us and other investigators is also incorporated into the discussion. The goal of the research described was to understand the underlying cause for these behaviors. Specifically, we asked:

What is the meaning of the behavior?

What is the meaning to the person suffering from dementia?

What is the meaning for the caregiver?

What is wrong about the behavior?

For example, a pacing behavior could be indicative of a resident's search for home, possibly the home that she grew up in. For the caregiver, her going in and out of rooms means disruption of other residents' routine and their peace of mind. Other possible reasons for the behaviors can span the range from neurological damage to unmet needs to environmental reinforcement, or an environmental trigger for the behaviors through understimulation or overstimulation. For this chapter, the emphasis is on describing disruptive behaviors, clarifying their meaning and etiology, and describing the therapeutic approaches suggested by the research findings.

INFORMANT RATING ASSESSMENT OF DISRUPTIVE BEHAVIORS

In order to study the behaviors, an assessment was developed in consultation with nursing staff members who were familiar with these behaviors. The assessment, the Cohen-Mansfield Agitation Inventory (CMAI), is schematically summarized in Figure 3.1. A caregiver who is familiar with a resident is asked to rate each behavior on a frequency scale from "never occurring" to "occurring several times an hour." Many other instruments have been developed to assess disruptive behaviors through caregiver ratings. These include the BEHAVE-AD (Reisberg et al., 1987), the Revised Memory and Behavior Problems Checklist (Teri et al., 1992), and the COBRA scale

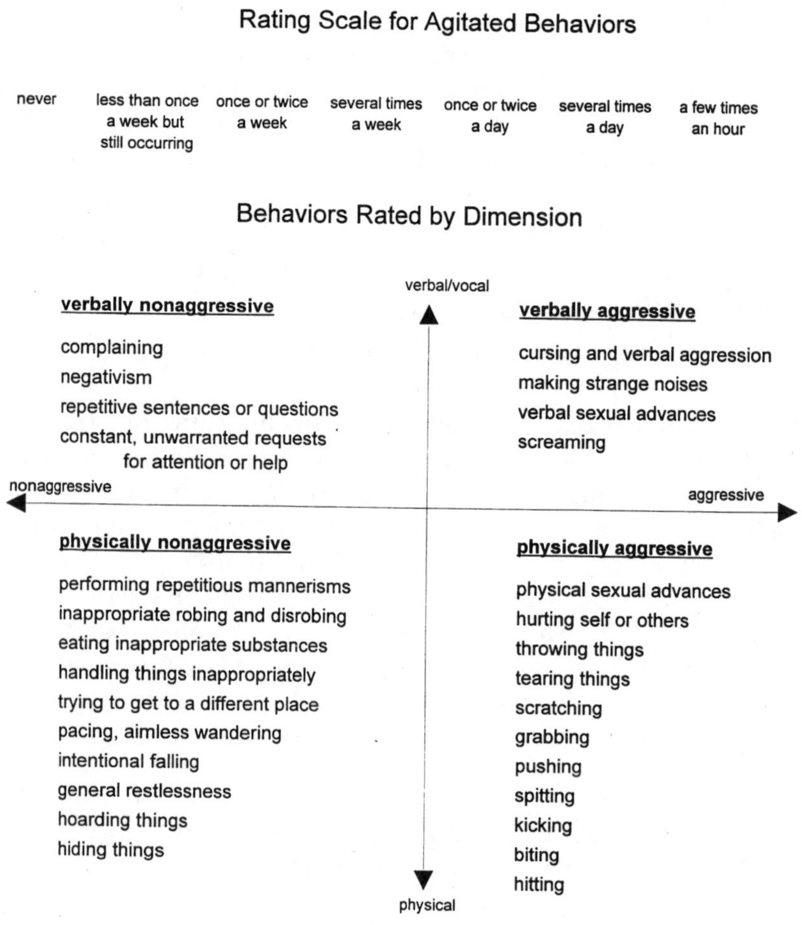

Rating Scale for Agitated Behaviors

never	less than once a week but still occurring	once or twice a week	several times a week	once or twice a day	several times a day	a few times an hour

Behaviors Rated by Dimension

verbal/vocal

verbally nonaggressive

complaining
negativism
repetitive sentences or questions
constant, unwarranted requests for attention or help

verbally aggressive

cursing and verbal aggression
making strange noises
verbal sexual advances
screaming

nonaggressive ◄————————————————————► aggressive

physically nonaggressive

performing repetitious mannerisms
inappropriate robing and disrobing
eating inappropriate substances
handling things inappropriately
trying to get to a different place
pacing, aimless wandering
intentional falling
general restlessness
hoarding things
hiding things

physically aggressive

physical sexual advances
hurting self or others
throwing things
tearing things
scratching
grabbing
pushing
spitting
kicking
biting
hitting

physical

FIGURE 3.1   CMAI—list of behaviors.

(Drachman, 1992). For a review of caregiver rating instruments, see Cohen-Mansfield and colleagues (1993).

THE PREVALENCE OF DISRUPTIVE BEHAVIORS

The most prevalent behaviors in the nursing home were verbal and physical nonaggressive behaviors, or specifically repetitive sentences or questions, constant requests for attention, pacing and wandering, negativism, complaining, and verbal aggression (Cohen-Mansfield, Marx, & Rosenthal, 1989). Reports of prevalence rates for pacing/ wandering range from 3% (Reisberg et al., 1987) to 59% (Rabins, Mace, & Lucas, 1982); rates for the category of noisy or disruptive verbal behavior range between 10 and 30% (Cohen-Mansfield & Deutsch, 1996); and the prevalence of aggressive behavior in institutional settings ranges from 8 to 91% (Cohen-Mansfield & Deutsch, 1996). The factors underlying so large a variance include disparities in the definitions of specific agitated behaviors, the method of observation, and the source of the report.

THE SYNDROMES OF AGITATION

In order to examine how these behaviors tend to occur together, we performed factor analyses on data describing 408 nursing home residents. The syndromes identified were as follows:

- *Aggressive behaviors*, including hitting, kicking, pushing, scratching, tearing things, biting, spitting, cursing, or verbal aggression
- *Physically nonaggressive behaviors*, including pacing, inappropriate dressing and undressing, trying to get to a different place, handling things inappropriately, general restlessness, repetitious mannerisms
- *Verbal and vocal agitated behaviors*, including complaining, constant requests for attention, negativism, repetitious sentences or questions, screaming

In a community-dwelling population of 200 participants of adult day care, verbally agitated behaviors were better described as two syndromes: *verbally aggressive behaviors,* including cursing, temper outbursts, screaming, and making strange noises, and *verbally nonaggressive behaviors,* including constant requests for attention, verbal bossiness or pushiness, complaining or whining, negativism, does not like anything, uncooperative, related interruptions, and unrelated interruptions (Cohen-Mansfield, Werner, Pasis, & Watson, 1995).

THE MEANING OF DISRUPTIVE BEHAVIORS

In order to clarify the meaning of disruptive behaviors, correlational studies were undertaken in which psychosocial, medical, and environmental factors were examined.

Psychosocial and Medical Correlates of Disruptive Behaviors

Psychosocial and medical correlates of agitation in the nursing home population are summarized in Figure 3.2. It is evident that the different types of agitation are related to distinct medical and psychosocial characteristics.

Verbally and vocally agitated individuals suffer from more medical conditions and higher levels of pain—as well as from depressed affect—than other nursing home residents, suggesting that these behaviors are associated with discomfort. Verbal and vocal agitated behavior were reported to be related to cognitive impairment in some studies (e.g., Reisberg, Franssen, Sclan, Kluger, & Ferris, 1989) but to the less cognitively impaired among the nursing home population in another study (Cohen-Mansfield, Marx, & Rosenthal, 1990). These findings can be explained by differences in the populations (i.e., people in the community are compared to a less cognitively impaired population than those who reside in the nursing home) and by the type of verbal/vocal agitation. Some types of verbal agitation (e.g., complaining) require the preservation of at least basic language skills, an ability that is absent in severe dementia. On the other hand, other types of vocal agitation, such as screaming, do not involve language skills and occur during late stages of dementia. Females are more likely to engage in verbally nonaggressive behavior (Cohen-Mansfield, Marx, & Werner, 1992), possibly reflecting consis-

Aggressive Behaviors

Male
Cognitive Impairment
Poor Quality of Social Relationships
Sleep Problems

Physically Nonaggressive

Cognitive Impairment
Moderate-to-High ADL Impairment
Relatively Good Health
Sleep Problems
Past Stress

Verbally Agitated

Females
Depression
Poor Health, Pain
Relatively Cognitively Intact
Poor Quality of Social Relationships
Sleep Problems

FIGURE 3.2   Correlates of agitated behaviors.

tent findings of greater verbal ability among females than males among all age groups.

People who engage in physically nonaggressive disruptive behaviors, in contrast with verbally agitated behaviors, have been reported to have fewer medical diagnoses and better appetites than other nursing home residents (Cohen-Mansfield et al., 1992). Being relatively healthy yet suffering from advanced dementia (Cohen-Mansfield, Culpepper, & Werner, 1995; Cohen-Mansfield et al., 1990), these persons may manifest physically nonaggressive disruptive behaviors as a form of stimulation when other types of stimulation are not available, because limitations imposed by dementia and by the nursing home environment restrict the older person's ability to utilize more appropriate types of stimulation. In a similar vein, individuals who pace or wander were reported to have been more active in earlier life (Monsour & Robb, 1982), although our research did not replicate that finding (Cohen-Mansfield et al., 1992). Some people who pace (one of the most common types of physically nonaggressive agitation) suffer from akathisia—an inner sense of restlessness—due to neurodegenerative disease or to an extrapyramidal reaction to antipsychotic or other drugs (Mutch, 1992).

Physically aggressive disruptive behaviors are more likely to be manifested by individuals with severe cognitive impairment (Cohen-Mansfield et al., 1990, 1995; Patel & Hope, 1992; Nasman, Bucht, Eriksson, & Sandman, 1993; Winger, Schirm, & Stewart, 1987; Meddaugh, 1987; Ryden, 1988; Swearer, Drachman, O'Donnell, & Mitchell, 1988). Physical aggression may be due to increased frustration due to decreased ability to communicate needs, as a result of which those needs are increasingly less likely to be met. It is also possible that the increased aggression among the more impaired is the result of greater organic brain deterioration, resulting in more behavioral disinhibition. The relationship between health and physically aggressive behavior is less clear. One study did not find significant relationships between health and aggressive behaviors in a nursing home population (Cohen-Mansfield et al., 1990), although another study reported a positive association between aggressive behavior and urinary tract infections (Ryden & Bossenmaier, 1988).

Males are more likely than females to exhibit aggressive forms of agitation (Marx, Cohen-Mansfield, & Werner, 1990; Ryden & Bossenmaier, 1988), a finding that corresponds to research indicating that males are more likely than females to engage in physical aggression among the population at large. Similarly, there are some indications that personality traits before the onset of dementia may make some persons more prone to manifest aggressive behaviors while suffering from dementia. Caregivers of 58% of the participants in a community-based study perceived aggressive behavior to result from premorbid personality (Spector & Jackson, 1994). Moreover, Ryden (1988) found a positive relationship between aggression prior to the onset of the dementing illness and performance on the Ryden Aggression Scale. Hamel et al. (1990) also found premorbid aggression to be a correlate of aggression in patients suffering from dementia. However, none of these studies was prospective.

Delusions and hallucinations were found to be related to all types of disruptive behaviors. (Cohen-Mansfield, Taylor, & Werner, 1998; Lachs, Becker, Siegal, Miller, & Tinetti, 1992; Steiger, Quinn, Toone, & Marsden, 1991; Deutsch, Bylsma, Rovner, Steele, & Folstein, 1991), although Swearer et al. (1988) did not find a correlation between the severity of hallucinations or delusions and assaultive behavior in their study of patients with various types of dementia. It is possible that the experience of a delusion or a hallucination causes internal discomfort, which is manifested in the disruptive behaviors. Alternatively, the same mechanisms which make a person prone to manifest disruptive behaviors are also in play when eliciting delusions or hallucinations.

Environmental Correlates of Disruptive Behaviors

Wandering and pacing occur most frequently in a corridor and near the nurses' station, where other people often spend time (Cohen-Mansfield, Werner, & Marx, 1992). In contrast to other agitated behaviors, wandering/pacing takes place under normal conditions of light, noise, and temperature rather than during uncomfortable environmental conditions. These findings are congruent with the notion that pacing and wandering may serve a self-stimulation purpose and not be a result of environmentally induced discomfort.

Vocally/verbally agitated behaviors are more likely to be manifested in the evening, when residents are alone, when they are physically restrained, or when they are involved in activities of daily living

(ADLs), especially toileting and bathing (Cohen-Mansfield, Werner, & Marx, 1990). Most screaming behavior (60%) has been found to be directed toward no particular person or object; 16% was directed toward a staff member and 11% toward an inanimate object. These environmental correlates support the notion that at least some verbally agitated behaviors are associated with discomfort, pain, or unmet social needs.

Physically aggressive behaviors have been reported to be a response to an intrusion of personal space by staff members or other residents (Bridges-Parlet, Knopman, & Thompson, 1994). Aggressive behaviors were observed more frequently in a social situation, at night when it was cold, or when the resident was in close contact with another person, such as during bathing. These individuals with advanced dementia respond in an aggressive manner in the presence of uncomfortable stimuli (when they are performing ADLs, or feeling cold) or when experiencing situations perceived as threatening (e.g., invasion of personal space) (Cohen-Mansfield & Werner, 1995).

Environmental Factors Associated With Disruptive Behaviors

Most disruptive behaviors (with the exception of pacing) were manifested more frequently when residents were physically restrained, when they were inactive or alone, when staffing levels were low, and when it was cold at night. In contrast, disruptive behaviors were less likely to occur when structured activities were offered, when music was on, or when social interaction with others was available (Cohen-Mansfield & Werner, 1995). These results concur with the hypothesis that agitated behaviors frequently signal discomfort and unmet needs.

THEORETICAL CONCEPTUALIZATION OF AGITATION

Based on the findings described above, agitated behaviors are conceptualized as resulting from an interaction between lifelong habits and personality, current physical and mental condition, and environmental factors both physical and psychological (Cohen-Mansfield & Deutsch, 1996) (Figure 3.3). More specifically, most agitated behaviors are manifestations of unmet needs. Because of the effects of dementia including a combination of perceptual problems, communication difficulties, and inability to manipulate the environment through appropriate channels, the elderly resident is unable to fulfill these needs. Disinhibition is an aggravating factor in the manifestation of these needs. The goal of treatment is to uncover the unmet need. Prior research established the connection between symptoms of agitated behavior and common causes eliciting this response. This, then, allows the clinician to expedite detection of the appropriate need and at times directs the clinician to appropriate interventions. The most common needs found are those for social and physical stimulation, both of which are lacking because of a combination of the effects of dementia, sensory deficits, and the monotony of the nursing home environment. However, other needs are often present, such as the need to avoid pain or hunger.

A related theoretical framework is that which concerns the concept of person-environment congruence (French, et al., 1974; Kahana, 1982) and that of the press-competence model (Lawton & Nahemow, 1973). These suggest that for optimal functioning, there must be a match between the person's needs and abilities and the demands of the environment as they relate to those needs and abilities. For any level of competence, there is a range of environmental demands that is favorable. The notion that lack of sufficient and appropriate stimulation is at the heart of certain types of disruptive behaviors and that the environment must be modified to match the person's stimulation needs and capabilities fits both those theoretical perspectives.

IMPLICATIONS OF PRIOR RESEARCH FOR THE TREATMENT OF DISRUPTIVE BEHAVIORS

Great variability has been found among elderly persons manifesting disruptive behaviors. This suggests that it may be necessary to individualize treatment to the specific needs and characteristics of each older person who manifests them. Great variability was also found within persons across time. This seems inherent to the manifestations

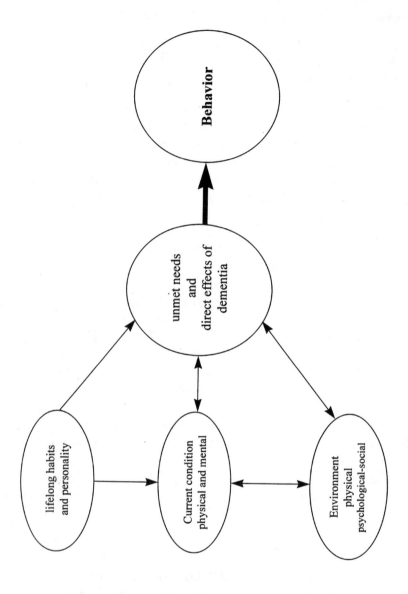

FIGURE 3.3 A model for explaining agitated behaviors.

of certain behaviors and to be a result of the response of other behaviors to environmental cues. It also underscores the importance of careful analysis in the determination of change following intervention.

The results of the studies described above suggest that different behaviors have different meanings. Most disruptive behaviors seem to signal discomfort. Some may be adaptive behaviors for the current mental and situational condition of the person. Other behaviors may signal an attempt to communicate wishes and needs when verbal communication is not available. Because many disruptive behaviors either communicate or signal discomfort and need, great caution is needed in their treatment. Disruptive behavior may at times be eliminated by medication, but if the underlying need persists, then the medication has obstructed final means of communicating this need. For example, if a person manifests a disruptive behavior such as screaming because of physical pain, a sufficiently large amount of psychotropic medication can cause the person to stop screaming. The disruptive behavior may then disappear, but the suffering probably lingers without any awareness on the part of the caregivers.

On a very concrete level, the results suggest that even the highly impaired person may be suffering when physically restrained, inactive, or alone. Therefore, social and structured activities are important components of care, even for the most demented segment of the nursing home population, who may not show any response to these stimuli.

CURRENT APPROACHES FOR THE TREATMENT OF AGITATION IN THE NURSING HOME

The harmful impact of disruptive behaviors on both nursing home caregivers and residents underscores the need to identify a means of treating agitation in the most effective way possible. Regrettably, the most common methods of treatment at present are the use of psychotropic medication and/or physical restraints (Fitz, Mallaya, & Roos, 1992; Rovner et al., 1996). These methods are frequently ineffective and involve adverse side effects, such as memory impairment, sedation, and tardive dyskinesia. Many other interventions have been described in the literature, including behavioral therapies (based on reinforcing desirable behavior and ignoring inappropriate behavior), music therapy, environmental changes, sensory stimulation (music and touch), decreased stimulation, validation therapy, activity programs, and relocation of the older person. For pacing and wandering, environmental modifications have been implemented, including locked or semi-locked doors, alarm systems, changed the exit areas (e.g., a grid on the floor in front of exit), or sheltered outdoor areas (for a more complete review of these strategies, see Cohen-Mansfield & Deutsch, 1996). However, most of the interventions were described as case studies, anecdotal clinical reports, or studies with very small sample sizes.

Rovner et al. (1996) conducted a controlled, randomized examination of interventions for behavioral problems associated with dementia. Nursing home residents either completed trials of a program called the "Activities, Guidelines for psychotropic medications, and Educational rounds (AGE) dementia care program" or else received their usual nursing home care. As its title suggests, the AGE program was made up of three components. The first was an activity program including music, exercise, crafts, relaxation, reminiscences, word games, and food preparation, with the goal of providing the residents with physical, mental, and social stimulation. The second component included guidelines for tapering or discontinuing psychotropic medications whenever possible. The third component involved a weekly meeting between AGE staff members and a psychiatrist to discuss each resident's behavioral, functional, and medical status. The AGE program successfully reduced behavioral disorders as well as psychotropic drug use and physical restraints.

TREATMENT ROUTES FOR EXPLORING AGITATION— THE TREA INTERVENTION

On the basis of prior findings, a model for intervention titled TREA (Treatment Routes for Exploring Agitation) has been developed. The assumptions underlying TREA are as follows:

- Treatment of disruptive behaviors needs to be individualized.
- The different syndromes of disruptive behaviors identified above have different etiologies and different meanings; therefore they require different approaches to treatment.

- Nonpharmacological approaches to treatment should precede pharmacological approaches.
- The first step in developing a specific treatment plan for a specific person is to attempt to understand the etiology of the agitated behavior or the need it signals.
- In developing a treatment plan, the remaining abilities, strengths, memories, and needs should be utilized, as well as recognition of disabilities, especially those in sensory perception and mobility. Unique characteristics of the individual—such as past work, hobbies, important relationships, and sense of identity—need to be explored to best match current activities to the person. (Examples of the range of possible activities to use as stimulation can be found in Zgola, 1987; Teri & Logsdon, 1991; Russen-Ronsdinone & DesRoberts, 1996).
- Prevention, accommodation, and flexibility are essential elements of intervention.

Prevention refers to structuring the environment in a manner that prevents the development of the needs that engender disruptive behaviors. Examples include better control of temperature, facilitation of activities, monitoring of pain, and provision of stimulation and social contact.

Accommodation involves ensuring that the design of the environment permits agitated behaviors to be manifested in a manner that fulfills the needs of the resident without imposing an undue burden on caregivers. For example, encouraging residents to pace and walk in a sheltered garden would allow them to manifest the behavior in an environment in which the behavior would be accepted as natural and which would not pose a risk to the resident or place a great burden on the caregiver (Cohen-Mansfield & Werner, 1998a). Similarly, providing pamphlets for residents to take and move around was used in one study (Cohen-Mansfield & Werner, 1998b) as an acceptable way of accommodating behaviors that would otherwise be labeled "inappropriate handling of things." Finally, even when the need is unclear, if the behavior is not harmful, it is frequently best accommodated. For example, an elderly woman was screaming next to the locked dining room door, obviously wanting to get in. Even though the room held no objects of interest or entertainment, the woman would neither be hurt nor cause harm if let in. Thus, simply accommodating a resident's wish without understanding it is frequently an appropriate route.

Flexibility refers to a willingness and ability of caregivers to adjust elements of the older person's daily routine to meet the resident's needs and/or wishes. Flexibility in meal-times, type of food (e.g., finger food vs. regular cooked food), sleep times, type of bathing (bath vs. wet-towel bathing) can all reduce the amount of conflict and its ensuing disruptive behavior by modifying the ADLs to accommodate the individual's needs, habits, moods, and tolerance.

The TREA approach is utilized to recognize needs by providing a series of questions, as delineated in Figures 3.4 to 3.6 for verbal disruptive behaviors, physically nonaggressive behaviors, and physically aggressive behaviors, respectively. Each figure guides the caregiver through the steps that must be explored in order to ascertain the need most likely contributing to the resident's manifested behavior.

Some of the etiologies to be uncovered are but a first step in further assessment. For example, if depressed affect is detected via self-report or by observation of facial expression (see Lawton et al., 1996), the reason for that affect must be ascertained. Indeed, social isolation is a common etiology for verbal agitation and may be related to the manifestation of depression as well. Similarly, delusions and hallucinations may be triggered by a decline in vision and hearing, which detracts from the ability to correctly interpret environmental stimuli. Alternatively, delusions may stem from actual environmental changes that have not been adequately explained to the person suffering from dementia (e.g., delusion of stealing the time of room change). These types of investigations need to be done in order to appropriately address the source of the verbally disruptive behavior.

VERBALLY AND VOCALLY DISRUPTIVE BEHAVIORS

Although there is some evidence suggesting that social isolation may be the most common need expressed by vocal and verbal disruptive behaviors (Cohen-Mansfield & Werner, 1997), for ethical rea-

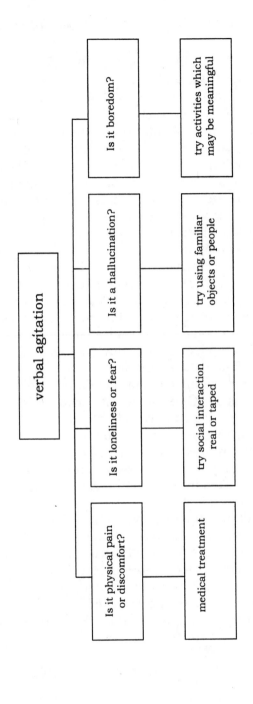

FIGURE 3.4 Approaches to management of verbal agitation.

sons, other needs should be ruled out first. The presence of pain and other physical discomfort, depressed affect, and delusions or hallucinations must be considered. Whereas the complete methodology of assessing these constructs in this population has not yet been established, some general rules should be followed, including the use of multiple sources of information, utilization of systematic observations, and manipulation of related environmental features. Examples of using multiple sources for determination of pain and discomfort could include asking family members about the types of pain the older person used to experience in the past, tests for urinary tract infection, and observation of whether behavior changed during change in body position.

Verbally disruptive behaviors seem to be most frequently related to social isolation; these behaviors decrease with the provision of appropriate ongoing social contact. In a study of verbally disruptive behaviors in the nursing home, both one-on-one social interaction and watching a videotape of a relative talking to the older person decreased verbal and vocal disruptive behaviors among residents who had manifested these behaviors at very high frequencies in comparison to a nonintervention condition (Cohen-Mansfield & Werner, in press a). One-on-one interaction was more effective, though also more costly. Individual differences were found, so that when all participants were exposed to both methods, some persons benefitted more from each of the interventions. This suggests that additional factors, such as the person's prior relationship with relatives, should be taken into account in customizing the specific program for each individual.

Some verbally disruptive behavior may serve a self-stimulatory function and may be associated with inactivity and boredom. Such behavior is likely to be reduced when structured activities are offered. In the study described above (Cohen-Mansfield & Werner, in press a), music chosen on the basis of the older person's past preferences significantly reduced verbally disruptive behaviors in comparison to a no treatment condition, though it was less effective than interventions aimed at social contact.

PHYSICALLY NONAGGRESSIVE BEHAVIORS

Although our research indicates that pacing and wandering, the most common type of physically nonaggressive behavior (Figure 3.5),

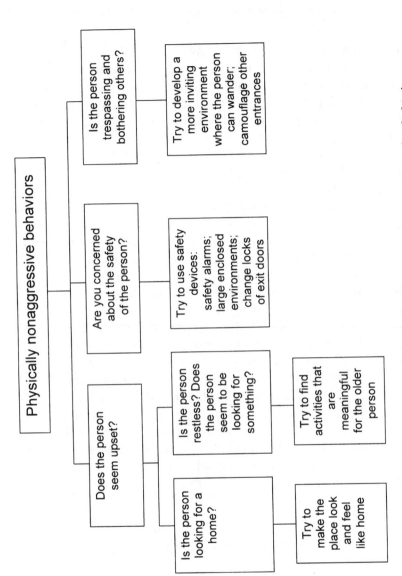

FIGURE 3.5 Approaches to management of physically nonaggressive behaviors.

are not associated with discomfort, as with verbally agitated behaviors, sources of discomfort need to be ruled out nonetheless. Clinically, some persons manifesting physically nonaggressive behaviors seem to be searching for something, usually something related to their past. Options for interventions include (1) changing the environment to resemble that for which the person is searching by displaying past pictures or furniture or (2) directing the person's attention to other comforting stimuli.

If the resident's behavior is not associated with discomfort, it is best accommodated. However, prior to simply allowing the older person to wander, several considerations must be addressed: namely the safety of the resident and the impact of his or her behavior on others. It is necessary to monitor residents so that they do not get lost. Technological devices like alarm systems can assist in assuring safety. The impact of their behavior on others frequently involves the older person wandering into other residents' rooms. Environmental modifications, including Velcro strips on doors or changing the appearance of doors, can decrease the incidence of trespassing. Finally, another obstacle to accommodating these behaviors is caregiver attitudes. At times these attitudes can be modified with appropriate education. When this is not feasible, the behavior of the older person must be directed into more acceptable channels, such as being asked to sort a specific heap of papers rather than just moving objects about, or being taken for a walk to a secure outdoor area rather than walking on her own. The utility of outdoor areas for some persons who tend to pace and wander has been demonstrated (Cohen-Mansfield & Werner, 1998a).

AGGRESSIVE BEHAVIORS

Aggressive behaviors (Figure 3.6) generally occur at a frequency much lower than that of other disruptive behaviors. A thorough functional analysis of the antecedents and consequences of several occurrences of the behavior is needed to clarify the most likely etiology. Additionally, the characterization of the behavior in terms of location, time of day, persons present, and persons toward whom the behavior is directed is helpful. Correlates found in the literature include physical discomfort, delusions, hallucinations, invasion of

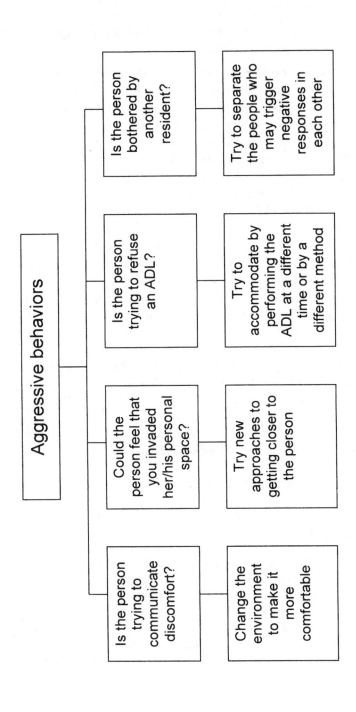

FIGURE 3.6 Approaches to management of aggressive behaviors.

personal space, or other intrusive activities by others—such as those related to performing ADLs, and irritation by another resident. Whereas some of the interventions would be straightforward (e.g., increase heating or provide additional clothing if the environment is cold), others, such as the provision of ADLs without triggering a sense of intrusion, are quite complex. These include caregiver training in approaching the older person in a different pace or manner, changing the environment in which the ADL is provided, or the frequency or method (e.g., bath vs. shower vs. sponge bath) by which it is administered. However, the methodology for optimal assistance in performance of ADLs has yet to be developed; this absence is probably the cause of a significant proportion of physically aggressive behavior in persons with dementia.

Managing disruptive behaviors of the elderly is a challenge to both formal and informal caregivers. The short analysis of the TREA approach underscores both the complexity of the behaviors, and, consequently, of their optimal management, as well as the creativity needed to find the solution that will match the older person's needs and level of disability to remaining abilities, sense of identity, and unique interests.

REFERENCES

Algase, D., & Tsai, J. (1991). Wandering as a rhythm. *The Gerontologist (Program Abstracts), 31,* 140.

Bridges-Parlet, S., Knopman, D., & Thompson, T. (1994). A descriptive study of physically aggressive behavior in dementia by direct observation. *Journal of the American Geriatrics Society, 42,* 192–197.

Cohen-Mansfield, J., & Billig, N. (1986). Agitated behaviors in the elderly: A conceptual review. *Journal of the American Geriatrics Society, 34,* 711–721.

Cohen-Mansfield, J., Billig, N., Lipson, S., Rosenthal, A. S., & Pawlson, L. G. (1990). Medical correlates of agitation in nursing home residents. *Gerontology, 36,* 150–158.

Cohen-Mansfield, J., Culpepper, W. J., & Werner, P. (1995). The relationship between cognitive function and agitation in senior day care participants. *International Journal of Geriatric Psychiatry, 10,* 585–595.

Cohen-Mansfield, J., & Deutsch, L. (1996). Agitation: Subtypes and their mechanisms. In S. Borson (Ed.), *Seminars in clinical neuropsychiatry.* Philadelphia: W. B. Saunders Company.

Cohen-Mansfield, J., Marx, M. S., & Rosenthal, A. S. (1989). A description of agitation in a nursing home. *Journal of Gerontology: Medical Sciences,* 44, M77–M84.

Cohen-Mansfield, J., Marx, M. S., & Rosenthal, A. S. (1990). Dementia and agitation in nursing home residents: How are they related? *Psychology and Aging,* 5, 3–8.

Cohen-Mansfield, J., Marx, M. S., & Werner, P. (1992). Agitation in elderly persons: An integrative report of findings in a nursing home. *International Psychogeriatrics,* 4, Supplement 2, 221–240.

Cohen-Mansfield, J., Taylor, L., & Werner, P. (1998). Delusions and hallucinations in an adult day care population: A longitudinal study. *American Journal of Geriatric Psychiatry,* 6, 104–121.

Cohen-Mansfield, J., & Werner, P. (1995). Environmental influences on agitation: An integrative summary of an observational study. *The American Journal of Alzheimer's Care and Related Disorders & Research,* (Jan/Feb), 32–39.

Cohen-Mansfield, J., & Werner, P. (1997). Management of verbally disruptive behaviors in nursing home residents. *Journals of Gerontology: Medical Sciences,* 52, M369–M377.

Cohen-Mansfield, J., & Werner, P. (1998a). Visits to an outdoor garden: Impact on behavior and mood of nursing home residents who pace. In B. J. Vellas, J. Fitten, & G. Fresconi (Eds.), *Research and practice in Alzheimer's disease intervention in gerontology.* Paris, France: Serdi.

Cohen-Mansfield, J., & Werner, P. (1998b). The effects of an enhanced environment on nursing home residents who pace. *Gerontologist,* 38, 199–208.

Cohen-Mansfield, J., Werner, P., & Marx, M. S. (1990). Screaming in nursing home residents. *Journal of the American Geriatrics Society,* 38, 785–792.

Cohen-Mansfield, J., Werner, P., & Marx, M. S. (1992). The social environment of the agitated nursing home resident. *International Journal of Geriatric Psychiatry,* 7, 789–798.

Cohen-Mansfield, J., Werner, P., Marx, M. S., & Lipson, S. (1993). Assessment and management of behavior problems in the nursing home setting. In L. Z. Rubenstein & D. Wieland (Eds.), *Improving care in the nursing home: Comprehensive reviews of clinical research* (pp. 275–313). Newbury Park, CA: Sage Publications.

Cohen-Mansfield, J., Werner, P., Watson, V., & Pasis, S. (1995). Agitation in participants of adult day care centers: The experiences of relatives and staff members. *International Psychogeriatrics,* 7, 447–458.

Deutsch, L. H., Bylsma, F. W., Rovner, B. W., Steele, C., & Folstein, M. F. (1991). Psychosis and physical aggression in probable Alzheimer's disease. *American Journal of Psychiatry,* 148, 1159–1163.

Drachman, D. A., Swearer, J. M., O'Donnell, B. F., Mitchell, A. L., & Maloon, A. (1992). The Caretaker Obstreperous-Behavior Rating Assessment (COBRA). *Journal of the American Geriatrics Society, 40,* 463–470.

Fitz, D., Mallya, A., & Roos, P. D. (1992). Psychotropic medications. *Hospital and Community Psychiatry, 43,* 1244–1245.

French, J. P. R., Rodgers, W., & Cobb, S. (1974). Adjustment as person-environment fit. In G. V. Coelho, D. A. Hamburg, & J. E. Adams (Eds.), *Coping and adaptation* (pp. 316–333). New York: Basic Books.

Hamel, B. A., Pushkar-Gold, D., Andres, A., Reis, M., Dastoor, D., Grauer, H., & Bergman, H. (1990). Predictors and consequences of aggressive behavior by community-based dementia patients. *Gerontologist, 30,* 206–211.

Kahana, E. (1982). A congruence model of person-environment interaction. In M. P. Lawton, P. G. Windley, & T. O. Byerts (Eds.), *Aging and the environment: Theoretical approaches* (pp. 97–121). New York: Springer.

Lachs, M. S., Becker, M., Siegal, A. P., Miller, R. P., & Tinetti, M. E. (1992). Delusions and behavioral disturbances in cognitively impaired elderly persons. *Journal of the American Geriatrics Society, 40,* 768–773.

Lawton, M. P., & Nahemow, L. (1973). Ecology and the aging process. In C. Eisdorfer & M. P. Lawton (Eds.), *Psychology of adult development and aging* (pp. 619–674). Washington, DC: American Psychological Association.

Lawton, M. P., Van Haitsma, K., & Klapper, J. (1996). Observed affect of nursing home residents with Alzheimer's Disease. *Journal of Gerontology: Psychological Sciences, 51B,* P3–P14.

Marx, M. S., Cohen-Mansfield, J., & Werner, P. (1990). A profile of the aggressive nursing home resident. *Behavior, Health, and Aging, 1,* 65–73.

Meddaugh, D. I. (1987). Aggressive and nonaggressive nursing home patients. *The Gerontologist, 27,* 127A.

Monsour, N., & Robb, S. S. (1982). Wandering behavior in old age: A psychosocial study. *Social Work, 27,* 411–416.

Mutch, W. J. (1992). Parkinsonism and other movement disorders. In J. C. Brocklehurst, R. C. Tallis, & H. M. Fillit (Eds.), *Textbook of geriatric medicine and gerontology* (p. 423). Edinburgh, Scotland: Churchill Livingstone.

Nasman, B., Bucht, G., Eriksson, S., & Sandman, P. O. (1993). Behavioral symptoms in the institutionalized elderly-relationship to dementia. *International Journal of Geriatric Psychiatry, 8,* 843–849.

Patel, V., & Hope, R. A. (1992). A rating scale for aggressive behaviour in the elderly—The RAGE. *Psychological Medicine, 22,* 211–221.

Rabins, P. V., Mace, N. L., & Lucas, M. J. (1982). The impact of dementia on the family. *Journal of the American Medical Association, 248,* 333–335.

Reisberg, B., Borenstein, J., Franssen, E., Salob, S., Steinberg, G., Shulman, E., Ferris, S. H., & Georgotas, A. (1987). BEHAVE-AD: A clinical rating scale for the assessment of pharmacologically remediable symptomology in Alzheimer's disease. In H. J. Altman (Ed.), *Alzheimer's disease: Problems and perspectives* (pp. 1–16). New York: Plenum Press.

Reisberg, B., Franssen, E., Sclan, S. G., Kluger, A., & Ferris, S. H. (1989). Stage specific incidence of potentially remediable behavioral symptoms in aging and Alzheimer's disease: A study of 120 patients using the BEHAVE-AD. *Bulletin of Clinical Neurosciences, 54*, 95–112.

Rovner, B. W., Steele, C. D., Shmuely, Y., & Folstein, M. F. (1996). A randomized trial of dementia care in nursing homes. *Journal of the American Geriatrics Society, 44*, 7–13.

Russen-Rondinone, T., & DesRoberts, A. M. M. (1996). STIR, Success through individualized recreation: Working with the low-functioning resident with dementia or Alzheimer's disease. *The American Journal of Alzheimer's Disease, 11*, 32–35.

Ryden, M., & Bossenmaier, M. (1988). Aggressive behaviors in cognitively impaired nursing home residents. *The Gerontologist, 28*, 179A.

Ryden, M. B. (1988). Aggressive behavior in persons with dementia living in the community. *Alzheimer's Disease and Associated Disorders, 2*, 342–355.

Spector, W. D., & Jackson, M. E. (1994). Correlates of disruptive behaviors in nursing homes, a reanalysis. *Journal of Aging and Health, 6*, 173–184.

Steiger, M. J., Quinn, N. P., Toone, B., & Marsden, C. D. (1991). Off-period screaming accompanying motor fluctuations in Parkinson's disease. *Movement Disorders, 6*, 89–90.

Swearer, J. M., Drachman, D. A., O'Donnell, B. F., & Mitchell, A. L. (1988). Troublesome and disruptive behaviors in dementia: Relationships to diagnosis and disease severity. *Journal of the American Geriatrics Society, 36*, 784–790.

Teri, L., & Logsdon, R. G. (1991). Identifying pleasant activities for Alzheimer's disease patients: The pleasant events schedule—AD. *Gerontologist, 31*, 124–127.

Teri, L., Traux, P., Logsdon, R., Uomoto, J., Zarit, S., & Vitaliano, P. P. (1992). Assessment of behavioral problems in dementia: The revised memory and behavior problems checklist. *Psychology and Aging, 7*, 622–631.

Winger, J., Schirm, V., & Stewart, D. (1987). Aggressive behaviors in long-term care. *Journal of Psychosocial Nursing, 25*, 28–33.

Zgola, J. M. L. (1987). *Doing things: A guide to programming activities for persons with Alzheimer's disease and related disorders.* Baltimore, MD: The Johns Hopkins University Press.

4

Psychotherapy with the Cognitively Impaired

Deborah Frazer

Conducting psychotherapy with cognitively impaired individuals has become a risky business. In May 1996, the Office of the U.S. Inspector General of the Department of Health and Human Services issued a report entitled *Mental Health Services in Nursing Facilities* (U.S. Department of Health and Human Services, 1996). Among the findings were that "in 32 percent of the records received Medicare paid for medically unnecessary services" (p. i). Lack of medical necessity was based on information about "the patient's condition, need for treatment, and ability to benefit from the treatment" (p. ii). In addition, the report states that "Those residents with a mental health diagnosis of dementia, including Alzheimer's disease, were more likely (58 percent) to receive questionable or unnecessary services than those with other diagnoses (45 percent)" (p. ii).

This report, and the denial of payments to providers that accompanied it, has left many clinicians unwilling to treat cognitively impaired individuals. Certainly some fraudulent and/or questionable practice has occurred, but the solution is not in refusing to treat or to pay for treatment of all impaired individuals in distress. Providers must become more knowledgeable about the psychiatric comorbidities of dementing disorders and more careful and selective about treatments they provide. Providers must continually assess need for services and the individual's therapeutic benefit from services. With this more knowledgeable and monitored therapeutic approach on the part of providers, the cognitively impaired can still receive the psychotherapeutic services they deserve.

In order to help therapists work with dementing clients, this chapter summarizes information on types and prevalence of cognitive impairment in the elderly. It discusses prevalence and course of comorbid depression and dementia. From a more anecdotal literature, the chapter discusses how a therapist might differentially experience clients with vascular versus Alzheimer's dementia. Teri and Logsdon's behavioral treatment for dementia with depression is reviewed, along with other modalities reported to be useful with this type of client. Finally, some therapeutic issues specific to the cognitively impaired are discussed.

DEFINITION OF COGNITIVE IMPAIRMENT

The National Institutes of Health declared the 1990s to be the "Decade of the Brain." By 1994, with the publication of the fourth edition of the *Diagnostic and Statistical Manual* (DSM-IV) (APA, 1994), the strong emphasis on the biological bases of behavior was evident. For those working with older adults, the most dramatic changes occurred in the reclassification of what had been called "organic mental disorders." The very term *organic* was dropped entirely from the DSM-IV "because it incorrectly implies that 'nonorganic' mental disorders do not have a biological basis" (p. 123). Therapists who were trained and who practiced in an earlier era can easily remember the almost casual assignment of the label "OBS" (organic brain syndrome) to many older adults—usually attended by a prescription for "no active treatment" or "custodial" care. The new classification reflects a growing sophistication about the complexities of brain function and dysfunction. It offers an opportunity for more finely tuned diagnosis, prognosis, and intervention with the cognitively impaired than did earlier classification.

The word *cognitive* derives from Latin and Greek words for "learn" and "know." Cognition is defined in the dictionary as the "mental process of knowing." Cognitive impairment implies difficulty with attention, perception, memory, learning, reasoning, abstraction, thinking, judgment, language function (aphasia), execution of motor activities independent of motor ability (apraxia), recognition and identification of objects independent of sensation (agnosia), and/or executive function (the ability to plan, initiate, sequence, monitor, and stop complex behavior). *Cognitive impairment* is a general term (not a DSM-IV diagnosis) referring to dysfunction in any or all of these areas and ranging from mild to severe.

Neuropsychological testing with standardized instruments is the most reliable and valid way to document the presence of cognitive impairment. An individual's performance is compared to "norms" or standards for the age group. Unfortunately, norms are not well developed for the very old or medically frail. Nor do they account for ethnic and cultural diversity. Therefore the most accurate way to assess an individual's cognitive status is to obtain a baseline assessment and retest after 8 or 12 months. Even if cognitive impairment is obvious without detailed neuropsychological testing, an initial diagnostic assessment is advisable to provide a baseline against which future assessments can be measured. Baseline assessments are especially useful in defining rehabilitation goals when an initially impaired individual suffers an additional brain insult such as a stroke or head injury from a fall. Comparison of subtests at baseline provides an assessment of areas of strength and weakness; comparison of the individual's second performance against the first performance provides an assessment of improvement or decline. In the case of degenerative dementias, baseline and yearly neuropsychological assessments can document the rate of decline, helping the family to predict and plan for caregiving needs, supervision requirements, and relocation to a more intensive care environment.

Many geriatric practitioners utilize some form of cognitive screening instrument, such as the Mini-Mental State Examination (Folstein, Folstein, & McHugh, 1975). While very useful for rough screening for impairment, these instruments are *not* sufficient for diagnostic purposes. Correctly utilized, mental status exams detect *possible* impairment or decline, providing the basis for referral for full neuropsychological evaluation.

TYPES OF COGNITIVE DISORDERS

Delirium

The three major categories of cognitive impairment in the elderly are delirium, dementia, and amnestic disorder. Delirium is character-ized by a disturbance in consciousness—i.e., a lack of awareness of the environment. The individual has difficulty focusing or sustaining attention. The condition develops rapidly, over a few hours or days. There may be impairment in other cognitive aspects, such as mem-ory, perception, or orientation. The condition often fluctuates over the course of the day. Delirium can be caused by a general medical condition such as infections, fluid or electrolyte disturbances, meta-bolic disturbances such as hypoglycemia, liver or kidney disorders, postsurgical reactions, or head trauma. Delirium also can be related to substance intoxication, withdrawal, medication interactions, or medication side effects. In the medically frail elderly, delirium may be due to a combination of a general medical condition and multiple medications being used to treat the condition. Delirium signals an acute, rapidly developing medical condition and should be consid-ered a medical emergency. Therapists who perceive a sudden change in cognitive status should immediately notify the client's physician.

Dementia

Dementia is characterized by the development (usually gradual) of multiple cognitive impairments, including memory impairment. It can be due to one or more of a number of neurological diseases or to the persisting effects of substance abuse, medications, or toxin exposure. The term *dementia* is derived from the Latin *de* (out) and *mens* (mind), or being "out of one's mind." Throughout history, the term implied a progressive and irreversible course. The most prevalent form of dementia among the elderly, dementia of the Alzheimer's type or DAT, is both progressive and irreversible. How-ever, the DSM-IV definition of dementia is based solely on symptom presentation and does not imply prognosis. Therefore, a dementia *can* be reversible, as in the case of medication-induced impairments.

The DSM-IV offers nine specific etiologies of dementia: Alzheimer's disease, cerebrovascular disease, human immunodeficiency virus (HIV) disease, head trauma, Parkinson's disease, Huntington's disease, Pick's disease, Creutzfeldt-Jakob disease, and persisting effects of a substance. In addition, dementia may be coded as due to other general medical conditions, multiple etiologies, or "not otherwise specified." All dementias must have evidence of multiple cognitive impairments, including memory impairment, and at least one of the following: aphasia, apraxia, agnosia, or a disturbance in executive functioning. It is not the intent here to provide detailed diagnostic criteria; the reader is referred to the DSM-IV (pp. 123–163) for specific diagnostic criteria and to Storandt and VandenBos (1994) for a fuller discussion of these conditions.

Amnestic Disorders

These disorders involve a set of conditions with the common characteristic of a circumscribed memory impairment. Unlike the dementias, amnestic disorders are not diagnosed when aphasia, apraxia, agnosia, or disturbance in executive functioning are present. Unlike delirium, amnestic disorders are not associated with problems focusing, sustaining, or shifting attention. Etiologies may include traumatic brain injury, stroke, or other cerebrovascular events; prolonged substance abuse or nutritional deficiency; neurotoxic exposure (such as carbon monoxide poisoning); or infections such as herpes simplex encephalitis.

Age-Related Cognitive Decline

This condition represents a new diagnostic category in DSM-IV. It is characterized by complaints of mild memory impairment (as for names or appointments) and increased difficulty in solving complex problems. However, neuropsychological testing reveals that cognitive function is within normal limits for the client's age. The differential diagnosis in this case is between age-related cognitive decline and an early presentation of dementia. Repeat testing after 1 year with no dramatic decline would support the diagnosis of age-related decline.

Mild Neurocognitive Disorder

It should be noted that this diagnostic category appears in Appendix B of DSM-IV (p. 706), which contains "criteria sets provided for further study." These research criteria sets are provided for researchers and clinicians who are interested in helping to refine the criteria and determine their possible utility. For this proposed disorder, the criteria include the presence of two or more mild cognitive deficits, documented by neuropsychological testing as an abnormality or decline, judged to be etiologically related to a neurological or general medical condition, and not meeting criteria for delirium, dementia or amnestic disorder. As with age-related cognitive decline, the most difficult differential diagnosis is to distinguish this category from an early dementia.

COMORBIDITY

Among the frail elderly, one frequently encounters comorbidities. That is, a 90-year-old client with cognitive impairment is less likely to demonstrate a "clear" presentation of a single etiology. She may have the gradual onset and progressive global decline typical of Alzheimer's disease but evidence hypertension, extremity weakness and on magnetic resonance imaging (MRI) findings that are consistent with vascular dementia. In addition, she may develop a comorbid delirium superimposed on the dementia due to a medication reaction. With advancing age, dementia due to multiple etiologies is more common. Additional difficulty with achieving diagnostic clarity with the frail elderly is occasional physician, family, and/or client resistance to pursuing the necessary tests to make an adequate diagnosis. As there is currently no "positive" marker for Alzheimer's disease, the diagnosis is made by ruling out all other possible central nervous or systemic competing diagnoses. These might include tumor, normal pressure hydrocephalus, subdural hematoma, hypothyroidism, or vitamin B_{12} deficiency. Neuropsychological testing, laboratory tests, and brain imaging are all required for an appropriate diagnosis yet are infrequently completed with frail elders. Nihilistic attitudes are expressed such as, "She probably only has a few years to live anyway—let her enjoy them in peace." This informal "rationing" of diagnostic health care prohibits frail elders and their families from making informed decisions about possible treatment alternatives and making appropriate care plans based on a accurate diagnosis. In the case of delirium, an unidentified or inaccurate diagnosis can be fatal. A therapist working with the cognitively impaired can advocate for appropriate initial diagnostic evaluations and regular re-evaluations to document the course of the illness and reveal any superimposed condition.

PREVALENCE OF COGNITIVE IMPAIRMENT

Estimates of the prevalence of cognitive impairment vary widely with age, subject location (institutional vs. community), disease severity, and specificity, and choice of measures contributing to the variability.

Evans et al. (1989) reported on the prevalence of probable Alzheimer's disease in a community-residing population. They found a prevalence rate of 3% in the 65- to 74-year-old group, 18.7% in the 75- to 84-year-old group, and 47.2% in those over age 85. This study is generally thought to represent the upper end of dementia prevalence estimates. Averaging prevalence estimates of dementia across studies, Cummings and Benson (1992) reported that an average of 6% of individuals over age 65 have severe dementia and an additional 10 to 15% have mild or moderate dementia. Prevalence of dementia increases with age and with institutional location (nursing home or hospital). Although estimates vary on the proportion of dementia cases accounted for by specific diseases, Alzheimer's disease seems to account for approximately 60 to 70% of cases and vascular dementia for approximately 10 to 15% (U.S. Department of Health and Human Services, 1996).

PRESENTATION OF DEMENTIA

Much work has been done to identify the stages of Alzheimer's disease. Reisberg, Ferris, and Franssen (1985) developed a model of staged functional decline, which assumes that the disease progresses in a predictable and orderly fashion. Other researchers have posited a more variable course to the disease.

the therapist, identification of the particular constellation of cognitive strengths and deficits can have a significant impact on therapeutic strategy. This pattern of strengths and deficits will be determined by the stage of the disease and by the type of dementia (e.g., Alzheimer's vs. vascular).

In Alzheimer's disease, the progression of deficits is from memory-specific to global impairment. In the latter stages, the individual is severely impaired in all cognitive functions. In contrast, in vascular dementia, the individual may exhibit "patchy" deficits, which reflect the specific areas of the brain in which blood circulation is compromised. The location and severity of the vascular disorder determine the type and severity of cognitive deficits.

The vascular "patchy" pattern is often more confusing and disconcerting to family members, staff, and inexperienced therapists. Even in the mild to moderate stages of Alzheimer's disease, caregivers may be confused by an uneven pattern of cognitive abilities and disabilities. It may be helpful for therapists and caregivers alike to think of an individual as "dement*ing*" rather than as "dement*ed*." The dementing diseases generally work their insidious destruction over many years. It is incumbent on the caregivers to continually recognize change in function and adapt treatment and care strategies to the new constellation of abilities and disabilities. Caregivers and therapists who follow dementing individuals over a long period of time may adapt so seamlessly and empathetically to the client's decline that they may fail to recognize and strategize for new disabilities.

PREVALENCE OF DEPRESSION AND ANXIETY IN THE COGNITIVELY IMPAIRED

Teri and Wagner (1992), reviewing empirical literature on comorbid depression and Alzheimer's disease, report that approximately 30% of Alzheimer's patients also meet DSM criteria for clinical depression.

Alexopoulos (1991) reported that 38% of geriatric psychiatric patients diagnosed as suffering from major depression also met criteria for an anxiety disorder. Rates were equivalent for those elderly with and without cognitive impairment. Parmelee, Katz, and Lawton (1993), combining clinical and subclinical anxiety, found prevalence rates of 10 to 17% in an institutional (nursing home and congregate housing) geriatric sample. These authors found high rates of comorbid depression, with 80% of the anxious respondents also evidencing depression. However, only 15% of those with major depression and 3% with minor depression displayed comorbid anxiety disorders. Therefore, the authors conclude that among the frail elderly, anxiety is a common aspect of a clear depressive syndrome, but it is incorrect to conclude that depression and anxiety are both facets of generally poor psychological well-being. Parmelee et al. found that persistently anxious persons were the most cognitively and functionally impaired. Nursing home residents displayed higher frequencies of anxiety than did apartment residents, reflecting the greater functional and cognitive impairment in the nursing home. This is in contrast to work (Parmelee, Katz, & Lawton, 1989) that found little relationship between depression and cognitive impairment in an institutional geriatric population.

PSYCHOTHERAPY WITH COGNITIVELY IMPAIRED CLIENTS: DYNAMIC PERSPECTIVES

The use of verbal psychotherapy with dementing clients can be controversial. If a client has difficulty remembering material from session to session, how can therapy work? If clients cannot abstract, how can they utilize insight? If the dementing disease is progressive and irreversible, are therapists seeking improvement not deluded if not outright unethical? More commonly accepted practices with dementing persons are therapeutic support for family members (Zarit & Zarit, 1982), socialization, and/or "adjunctive" therapies such as music, art or recreation.

A few pioneering efforts have been made in the utilization of psychotherapy with dementing individuals. Verwoerdt (1981), writing from a psychoanalytic perspective, noted the tenacity of affective response in dementia, with consistency of affective style persisting long after cognitive resources are devastated. Transference was observed to develop rapidly, facilitating the ability to form relationships. Miesen (1992) utilizes Bowlby's attachment theory to understand the phenomenon of "parent fixation," or the belief that one's deceased parents are still alive. Attachment behaviors—such as crying, calling, and touching—are activated in unfamiliar ("strange") situations and when an individual is feeling unsafe or insecure. If the attachment behavior is unreciprocated, the individual will develop parent fixation. In the later stages of dementia, the feelings of insecurity become permanent, and the parent fixation is generated from within the individual to continuously provide a sense of security. From this perspective, one role of psychotherapy is to facilitate attachments that can ease the dementing person's anxiety stemming from being in a continuous "strange" situation.

Hausman (1992) also advocates utilizing psychodynamic psychotherapy with dementing elders. She notes the high prevalence of emotional disease—depression, anxiety, and paranoia—in dementia. The primary goals of dynamic therapy are to address such affective states through the experience of a caring relationship, emotional catharsis, and enhancement of self-esteem. In addition, clients may be able to minimize behavioral problems, increase coping skills, achieve a sense of control, and grieve over losses.

Hausman advocates working primarily in an affective rather than a cognitive mode, with attention to reflection of current feelings and past stories, feelings, and events. Transference is acted rather than interpreted, with the therapist being the strong parent or loving child, as needed. The therapist reflects and carries the client's past, permitting the client to let go of the need for constant repetition. Ventilation of feelings allows the client to move on, and making choices within sessions allows the client to move toward mastery.

Therapists who are new to work with dementing clients may be startled by the psychological growth that can occur in the midst of progressive cognitive deterioration. As the brain disease weakens earlier defenses, individuals may be able to experience a wider range of emotions, deeper relationships, and long-buried conflicts. A skilled therapist can facilitate the transformation of these "openings" into psychological growth rather than frightening or overwhelming experiences.

Jones (1995) applied the Sullivanian principles of interpersonal therapy inspired by Sullivan to therapeutic treatment of dementing elders. He notes the centrality of anxiety in Sullivan's theory and the role of the "self" in managing anxiety. The development of the self is characterized by decreasing egocentrism, increasing separation of self from nonself, and a growing appreciation of logical cause-and-effect relationships. With these developments comes the ability to negotiate the successful adult interpersonal relationships which are critical to manage or avoid anxiety.

In a progressive dementia, Jones notes that the self becomes increasingly regressed and unable to negotiate the interpersonal world successfully. In the early stages of dementia, when the patient is aware of deficits, therapy may be oriented toward helping him or her utilize premorbid coping mechanisms to manage anxiety and fear. Slowly, the disease process creates more anxiety by increasing deficits and decreasing coping mechanisms. In the late stages of dementia, the anxiety may be manifested by repetitive motor activities and questions, hoarding, "catastrophic reactions," and other problem behaviors associated with moderate to severe dementia. The therapist's task, in this model, is to help the patient manage anxiety. This may be done through application of greater or lesser environmental stimulation (Parmelee & Lawton, 1990) and through the anxiety reduction inherent in a supportive, established relationship.

PSYCHOTHERAPY WITH COGNITIVELY IMPAIRED: A COGNITIVE-BEHAVIORAL MODEL

When clients exhibit both depression and dementia, the therapists may be uncertain about the etiology of either condition. The cognitive impairment could be considered a result of the depression ("pseudodementia" or "dementia syndrome of depression"). The depression could be viewed as a psychological reaction to the cognitive loss. The two disorders could be completely independent of each other. Finally, the depression and dementia could be manifestations of the same process of destruction of brain tissue. While research into the psychological and biological relationships of depression and dementia continues, the therapist is encouraged to treat the depression in this population as aggressively as in any other. As with other clients, if the depression is refractory to psychological treatments, consultation for medication or other biological treatments is advised.

Teri and Gallagher-Thompson (1991) have outlined a structured cognitive and behavioral treatment program for depression in cognitively impaired clients. Although the authors focus on depressed

Alzheimer's disease patients, the techniques are applicable to any cognitively impaired older adult who has been medically assessed and treated for reversible conditions. Teri and Gallagher-Thompson's strategies draw upon Beck's cognitive theory of depression (Beck, Rush, Shaw, & Emery, 1979) and Lewinsohn's behavioral approach (Lewinsohn, Antonuccio, Steinmetz, & Teri, 1984). They assume that the client and family have received a thorough cognitive evaluation and feedback, understanding that the goal of therapy is to improve not cognition but rather the associated depression and "excess" disability. They also recommend that therapists provide a good deal of structure to each session.

Cognitive therapy is recommended for clients suffering from depression in the early stages of a dementing illness. The goal is to challenge negative cognitions, reduce cognitive distortions, and help the client generate more adaptive cognitions. Second, the therapist encourages the client to assume a sense of control over moods and life situations.

In this model, clients are seen for 16 to 20 individual sessions, with occasional contact with family members to enlist their support. Sessions are highly structured, using standard cognitive treatment of depression: recording dysfunctional thoughts and accompanying negative feelings; challenging dysfunctional cognitions and replacing them with more adaptive interpretations; and rating and analyzing the cognition-mood relationships to understand how adaptive thoughts can lead to improved mood.

Teri and Gallagher-Thompson review adaptation of standard cognitive therapy for the mildly cognitively impaired: homework assignments must be simple; clients are provided with homework folders, note pads for in-session notes, and audiotapes of sessions to review; sessions are briefer and more frequent (30 minutes twice per week); and termination is spread over 1 to 2 months, with scheduled booster sessions to help with dependency and fear of losing the supportive relationship.

For the more moderately or severely cognitively impaired client, the depression is addressed through behavioral strategies. Based on the theory that depression is sustained and increased through reinforcements, the therapist's goal is to intervene in the reinforcement contingencies in a way that would stimulate nondepressive behaviors and reduce depressive behaviors. This is accomplished by increasing the level of positive and decreasing the level of negative activities and events. Interviews are targeted to both client and caregiver, with the importance of the caregiver's participation increasing as the level of dementia increases.

The initial sessions with client and caregiver are used to explain the treatment rationale, gain agreement for the strategy, and establish a basis for hopefulness regarding alleviation of the depression.

The therapist proceeds by teaching behavior-change principles to the caregiver and, if possible, the client. These include identification of a problem, specification of conditions (time, location, persons present, etc.), and planning, evaluating, and modifying an intervention. Caregivers are taught to cope with behavioral disturbances as well as to increase the frequency and duration of pleasant events each day. By learning to track and analyze behaviors and mood, caregivers learn how depressive mood can be alleviated by increasing positive events and decreasing unpleasant events. Therapists may find the Pleasant Events Schedule-AD (Teri & Logsdon, 1991) useful, or they may construct their own lists of pleasant activities.

The advantage to the cognitive-behavioral approaches outlined above are the clarity of focus, time-limited scope, and strong theoretical rationale. If clients and caregivers are persuaded that the rationale is sensible and the interventions are feasible, the therapist will have established therapeutic optimism and commitment to proceed with the outlined course of treatment. Difficulties may arise, however, if the client or caregiver does not accept the theoretical premise of cognitive-behavioral treatment. For example, the negative cognitions experienced in early dementia may be entirely realistic and appropriate. Rather than replacing these negative beliefs about the disease and the future, a client may need to fully experience the fear, the anxiety, and the sense of loss before being able to grieve and finally adapt.

In the clinical experience of this author, the cognitive-behavioral approaches are excellent adjuncts to more individually tailored therapy. Frail clients and their families are often impatient or noncompliant with elaborate homework, tracking, or monitoring systems. However, the underlying principles can be applied easily and with great success; encouraging discussions of adaptation and coping, enhancing a sense of control, and altering the environmental contingencies to decrease problematic situations and increase pleasure for both client and caregiver. One is often struck how clients and caregivers describe their lives only in terms of greater or lesser burden. Simply introducing the concept of pleasure—and the importance of pleasure in the lives of *both* client and caregiver—can provide a breakthrough of hope for better days.

PSYCHOTHERAPY WITH COGNITIVELY IMPAIRED CLIENTS: THE E-I-E-I-O MODEL

Recent research has shown that cognitively impaired individuals do not respond well to mnemonic strategies (Camp & McKitrick, 1992; Camp et al., 1993; Howard, 1991). Explaining this phenomenon by drawing upon research on memory subsystems, Camp et al. (1993) distinguish between "explicit" memory ("declarative" memory in some schema) and "implicit" memory ("nondeclarative" or "procedural" in some schema). Explicit memory involves conscious, effortful attempts to remember the new nursing assistant's name; time orientation (day, date, month, year); a list of words presented 10 minutes previously; or a short grocery "list" committed to memory with hopes of retrieving it upon arrival at the store. Implicit memory is captured by the phrase "It just comes back" or "Some things stay with you forever." Examples include remembering religious rituals when "primed" by music or smells; remembering how to play the piano or ride a bicycle by starting to do it; remembering the words of a song while singing it. Explicit memory has been shown to decline with age and to be devastated in Alzheimer's disease and other dementias. Implicit memory, however, may be more spared.

Camp distinguishes between two types of information storage: internal and external. In internal storage, individuals attempt to retain and recall information through internal cognitive means. Retention may be consciously intentional ("I've got to remember this name or phone number") and aided by internal mnemonics (the HOMES acronym for the Great Lakes). In contrast, external storage entails the utilization of devices or aids to carry information outside the person. Examples of external storage are appointment books, calendars, written shopping lists, medication dispensers, or an umbrella left hanging on the doorknob at night when rain is expected the next day. Camp posits that internal information storage and recall is more effortful and more impaired with age and disease; external information storage is less dependent on full cognitive capacity and high motivation. In later stages of dementia, even external storage mechanisms may break down because individuals must remember to use the devices or aids.

Putting together the internal versus external types of storage and explicit versus implicit types of memory, Camp proposed a model for memory training. In this model, individual memory training requires the most effort and is most likely to be unsuccessful in a dementing illness. However, the model provides a strategy for taking advantage of the least damaged systems in a cognitively compromised population: utilizing implicit memory systems with internal or external storage. To utilize implicit memory, Camp suggests classical conditioning techniques and motor and verbal priming, based on work by Squire (1992).

Classical conditioning involves pairing an existing stimulus-response bond with a new, conditioned stimulus. In Camp's example, an African-American male, new to an adult day care center, was being verbally abused by a small group of demented white females. Verbal discussion, reprimand, or prohibition of the abusive language had no effect, as the females could not retain the discussions or rules. The successful intervention consisted of pairing an identified positive stimulus (rewards, treats, honors) with the new resident: i.e., he became the one to pass out the "goodies" in hopes of developing a conditioned positive response. In this single case report, the female clients soon became positively disposed toward the new resident and verbal abuse diminished significantly. This was accomplished at the unconscious, implicit level, with the females being unable to report why they had come to like their new colleague. They did not remember that they had previously felt differently toward him.

The use of this model and an accompanying spaced-retrieval memory technique reported previously (Camp & Stevens, 1990) offer psychotherapists a framework for strategies to help the cognitively impaired individual cope with the effects of the impairment in daily living. In our applications of teaching external aids for information storage, we have found that the use of these aids should be initiated early in the disease process and be accompanied by set motoric rituals. For example, by pinning a "to-do" calendar to the back of the front door of a senior apartment, one "pairs" the habit of looking at the calendar, making entries and retrieving reminders, and exiting the apartment for meals. If this behavior is conditioned early in the dementia, it can provide an external information storage system that will last quite far into the progression of the disease. Similarly, if a client can be conditioned early in the disease to play back a therapy tape when he or she is feeling confused or anxious, this behavior may provide anxiety reduction late into the disease process. Trying to initiate such anxiety-reduction techniques in the late stages of dementia for the first time seems to produce only frustration and confusion about how to use the audio equipment.

GROUP PSYCHOTHERAPY WITH THE COGNITIVELY IMPAIRED

Group approaches with the cognitively impaired can have a powerful influence on clients' affective and behavioral lives. Group therapy can range from a traditional, low-intensity service of once-weekly 1-hour sessions to the high-intensity service of partial psychiatric hospitalization, which may consist of up to five group sessions daily. Unfortunately, need for service is not always neatly correlated with appropriateness for service: very disturbed clients who may need the high-intensity partial hospitalization service may be too disruptive to be seen in a group therapy modality. The clients may benefit from individual treatment oriented to improving social behavior to the point of where group therapy is tolerated.

Burnside and Schmidt (1994) recount how a leader of a cognitively impaired group may need to function, in contrast to a leader of a nonimpaired group. The group leader must have realistic expectations, observe carefully to note signs of progress, be prepared to meet the dependency and affectional needs of members, and personally provide stimulation to counter the lack of emotion, energy, and initiative among the impaired group members.

Therapists at the Philadelphia Geriatric Center have experimented with a variety of group structures and formats with dementing residents. The foci of the groups have ranged from highly structured psychoeducational groups (coping with stress; social skills training; coping with memory loss) to relatively unstructured groups that vary with the client's issues and goals (adjusting to recent medical events; improving positive affect).

Finding the "right" structure and format seems to be an interactive process between therapist and clients. Just as "older adults" are a heterogeneous group, the "cognitively impaired" bring widely varying personalities, behaviors, cognitive strengths and weaknesses, and affective strengths and problems to the group therapy situation. Within reason, heterogeneity can serve to keep a group lively, and members can benefit from differences as well as shared problems. In the same way, therapists vary in their affective levels, comfort with directiveness, ability to be spontaneous, and tolerance for the often slow progress observed in the cognitively impaired. We have found that the first task of conducting group therapy with the cognitively impaired is for therapists to develop self-awareness about their own strengths and weaknesses as group leaders. From there, therapists assess the needs and issues confronting the group of cognitively impaired; finally, they decide upon a format and structure to address the therapeutic issues that takes full advantage of their own individual style.

The only group therapy format we have found to be notably unsuccessful in achieving its goals was a memory skills training group for mildly to moderately cognitively impaired tenants in a senior apartment complex. The therapists found the group members unable to utilize the mnemonic strategies and too memory-impaired to complete homework assignments or even to remember to bring materials to the group each week. The group members did report highly favorable responses to the group sessions as a forum to discuss their memory difficulties without shame, to establish relationships with others suffering from a common malady, and to reduce their anxiety about their impairment and their future.

PSYCHOTHERAPY WITH COGNITIVELY IMPAIRED CLIENTS: COMMON ISSUES

Whether a therapist utilizes a psychodynamic, cognitive-behavioral, or experimental approach, certain issues or themes are likely to surface in verbal psychotherapy with the cognitively impaired. Three common themes are loss, adaptation, and interpersonal conflict.

Although these same themes may arise for the non-cognitively impaired, they have a unique meaning in dementia.

Loss

This is a frequent theme in any aging population. With advancing years, clients suffer loss of family and friends, physical abilities, and perhaps income, housing, or status. In a dementing individual, loss may entail the actual loss of one's self or one's identity. What begins by forgetting the names of grandchildren can end with forgetting one's occupation throughout life, forgetting a 60-year marriage, or forgetting one's own children. In the early to middle stages of dementia, clients regularly sense their memories—their very selves—slipping away. This type of loss is attended by great anxiety. In the late stages of the disease, clients frequently lose awareness of their deficits and thus may be less disturbed by the profound loss of "self" than their caregivers or families may be. Yet even in very late dementia, some clients may experience moments or hours of self-awareness (particularly in the more variable vascular dementia). In these moments, the individual may achieve enough self-awareness to be cognizant of the extent of his or her losses. The grief and anxiety are profound. Therapists may hear phrases such as, "Is this what I've become?" or "Am I like them?" (pointing to other demented residents). Helping dementing individuals cope with the loss of their sense of self has some elements in common with preparing for death, but without the finality. It can be a time of great anguish for the client and for the therapist, yet the power of the therapeutic relationship can be of enormous value. The therapist's verbal or nonverbal message is a simple one, "You are not alone." Yet this simple message may be enough to allow the individual to pass into a stage of the disease where self-awareness is blessedly limited.

Adaptation

In tandem with loss comes adaptation. Despite earlier declarations that persons with dementia could not learn new information, we now recognize that new learning does occur, probably in the "implicit" memory system described above. Those who have worked in nursing homes can attest to the ability of seriously demented residents to learn which nursing assistants they like best and which nursing assistants they definitely do not like. These impaired individuals may never learn the names of any assistants, but they will learn and demonstrate preferences. Cognitively impaired persons are often required to make major adaptations. They may change residences, go to and from hospitals, and be required to adapt to a large number of in-home or institutional caregiving staff (who may have frequent turnover). Accomplishing this adaptation with limited cognitive resources may be too taxing for the impaired individual. Examples of unsuccessful adaptation abound: resistance to care, aggressive behavior, pacing, calling out, attempting to "escape," or complete withdrawal. The cognitively impaired person may not have the language capability to express difficulty with the adaptive process. The role of the therapist in this situation is to assess the client's maladaptive behaviors and affect and to develop a strategy to ease the process of adaptation. This may involve mediating between the client and the family or institutional caregivers to develop a care plan that is less demanding on the client's limited resources for adaptation. For example, if a client is very resistive to personal care in a new residential setting, the therapist may discern that the client is upset by the large number of "strangers" providing intimate care. The therapist may be able to elicit from the client, verbally or by observation, which assistant is the "favorite" caregiver. The therapist may then be able to negotiate with the nursing staff that this client would have a primary caregiver (a single assigned nursing assistant) for at least the first several weeks of his or her new residence.

In earlier stages of dementia, the adaptation process can be more verbal. Having an opportunity in therapy to complain about adapting to a roommate in a nursing home may prevent an individual from acting out distaste for the roommate directly.

With a cognitively impaired client, therapists may need to "lend" their own cognitive abilities to the client to help compensate, much as they would help to read something for a blind client or interpret sound for a hearing-impaired client. How would this work? An impaired client may have little "executive function"—i.e., the ability to plan, initiate, and follow through on a strategy. Perhaps the therapist and client determine that a client's depression is related to the inability to establish new friendships in a facility. Despite verbal discussions, role playing, and other traditional therapeutic techniques to encourage adaptive behavior, the client is unable to initiate the appropriate strategy. With the client's permission, the therapist may substitute his or her own "executive function" by approaching the care team and eliciting suggestions for a "friend for the client." That friend would be best matched if he or she had complementary strengths and deficits; e.g., perhaps the friend was good at taking initiative but was vision-impaired. The care team would follow through on the strategy for relationship building, perhaps by seating these friends together at meals or activities. In other therapeutic contexts, this approach would seem patronizing or dependency-promoting. With a cognitively impaired individual, however, it is an accurate recognition of deficits and provision of compensatory environmental supports to aid in the process of adaptation.

Interpersonal Conflict

Interpersonal conflict, like adaptation, is by no means limited to the cognitively impaired. However, the sources of conflict and the resources for resolving conflict are unique to persons with dementia. Interpersonal tension often can be traced to one of three root causes: the struggle to maintain control; disinhibition; or confusion.

Within the broad concept of struggling to maintain control are numerous arenas for conflict. A client may be enraged by family members' insistence that she move from her lifelong home to a more supervised setting. A client may be convinced that family members are trying to steal his money when they assume financial guardianship. A client may interpret a caregiver's attempts to help with bathing, dressing, or toileting as an invasion of her privacy and her personal space. A client may misplace a pocketbook and angrily accuse family members, staff or a roommate of stealing it. In each case, the client may experience the ebbing of personal competence and blame others as a way of defending self-esteem, dignity, and autonomy. As control is increasingly lost by the client, she may exhibit desperate, irrational attempts to retain it. No amount of rational discussion will convince a frightened, angry dementing person that giving up more control is the "right" thing to do. Rather, the therapist can empathize with the loss, help the client to grieve it, and work with the client's team to provide the greatest number of opportunities for choice and control that can be managed. As larger, more complex areas such as financial management must be transferred, the client can retain some control through regular briefings on financial status and check signing. Even if the client cannot fully comprehend the financial discussion, she *will* comprehend that she is being included. As always, clients are variable in their needs and preferences. Therapists can be extremely helpful by assessing which, if any, control or autonomy areas most heavily affect the client's psychological well-being and devising a plan that addresses those needs.

A second significant source of interpersonal conflict among the cognitively impaired is the degradation of socially appropriate behavior. Complex social behavior may suffer in some forms of dementia, with an inability to actively socialize in positive ways and an increased tendency to exhibit behaviors considered antisocial by others. Examples in a residential facility include rummaging through others' drawers, getting into others' beds, touching others on the face or arms, and taking food from others' plates or trays. In a home setting, the degradation of social skills can be particularly unsettling for a spouse, who is progressively "losing" a lifelong companion. In one marriage counseling example, the wife of an early-stage dementing man expressed a great deal of anger toward her husband because he could no longer discuss the *McNeil-Lehrer News Hour* with her. In another marriage counseling example, the wife of a late-stage dementing man had physically abused him because she was so frustrated by his verbal unresponsiveness. The therapist, as a skilled communicator, can assess the client's remaining strengths and deficits in communication and teach caregivers how to maximize remaining social strengths. The therapist can teach good communication skills to caregivers, training them to focus more on doing and less on talking, and helping them to lower their expectations for client responsiveness.

For clients whose socially inappropriate behavior leads to conflict with other residents, environmental modifications are usually the most successful interventions. Therapists can suggest taping red crepe paper across another resident's doorway to discourage entry. Locked drawers prevent rummaging. Distant seating at meals prevents "stealing" of food. Clients, staff and family members need to know that discussions, threats, rules, and punishment will not change these socially inappropriate behaviors. The impaired client simply does not have the explicit memory capacity to learn, retain, and recall these rules and consequences. Prevention and avoidance of potentially conflictual situations are far more likely to produce success.

A third source of interpersonal conflict among the cognitively impaired is the disinhibition of inappropriate social behavior. Although the focus of this chapter is not behavior management, the interpersonal aspect of this condition are covered here. At some point in their lives, most people experience thoughts or fantasies of aggressive or sexual behavior. As socialized, civilized human beings, we inhibit these thoughts and fantasies, pushing them "out of our minds" or relegating them to private fantasy times. Some dementing individuals suffer a noticeable inability to control their sexual or aggressive impulses and will act on them in the presence of others. This is referred to as *dis*inhibited behavior and may include sudden aggressive outbursts, public masturbation, or grabbing breasts or genitalia of caregivers.

Disinhibited behavior is particularly disturbing to others because it violates deep social taboos. It can also be frightening, dangerous, painful, and embarrassing. It is by nature unpredictable. Punishment has no effect, as by definition this is impulsive, unconsidered behavior. It can elicit very angry feelings in caregivers which, if expressed verbally or physically, can increase clients' agitation. Insight, behavior contracts and traditional operant behavior modification do not seem successful in controlling disinhibited behavior. In the past, nursing homes have often "treated" these individuals with large doses of major tranquilizing agents. Under OBRA (the Omnibus Budget Reconciliation Act of 1987) regulations, this is no longer an acceptable approach.

What approaches *do* work? Again, the best chance for success is prevention and avoidance of situations that seem to elicit or "set off" the behavior. The therapist, in cases of disinhibition, becomes a detective to analyze the behavioral "triggers." Time of day, personnel, location, and events are recorded and interpreted to reveal connections to the behavior. When a pattern emerges, the therapist can help the team develop a plan to prevent or avoid trigger situations, provide alternative outlets for the sexual or aggressive impulses, and calm staff or family response should such behavior occur. Lowering the frequency of incidents is the goal. In one ongoing case of sexually inappropriate touching of staff by a disinhibited male resident, the therapist utilized multiple approaches ranging from increasing visit time by his wife (an inhibiting factor); increasing activities (for distraction and to "tire" him); and provision of a stuffed animal (for comfort and kinesthetic stimulation). In addition, significant work was done with staff to let them ventilate their negative feelings about the behavior, encourage continued behavior tracking, and continued solicitation of suggestions for prevention.

PSYCHOTHERAPY WITH COGNITIVELY IMPAIRED CLIENTS: PRACTICAL ISSUES

The major therapeutic modifications with this population address deficits of memory and attention. When the client exhibits difficulty with sustaining attention to the therapeutic tasks, the therapist has several options. First, try allowing a 5-minute "breather" from sustained therapeutic dialogue. Look at family photographs or chat about less emotionally laden subjects. Second, increase the therapist's stimulation levels: move closer, speak more loudly, use more gestures. Third, change modalities: instead of talking, have the client write, draw, paint, or sing about the therapeutic theme for a few minutes. Fourth, change locations: move to a different room, office, or out of doors. Finally, if it becomes evident that a client simply cannot work for a full 45- to 50-minute session, consider substituting two shorter sessions.

Strategies to compensate for memory loss have been mentioned in relation to specific models above, but many can be applied across all approaches. The primary compensatory aid involves the same advice given to younger individuals experiencing "normal" memory loss: "Write it down!" This may mean keeping a therapy log or journal, with entries at the end of each session that are reviewed at the beginning of the next. For more detailed work, a client can jot down notes during the course of a session and the therapist can utilize the notes to keep the discussion focused and for summary and review at the end of the session. Audio- or videotapes also can be used for recording and reviewing. Reminder notes about particular issues can be posted in a client's room, apartment, or house. Calendars can be filled in with events, both past and future, to reflect back to the client the continuity of life rather than the moment-to-moment experience of the memory-impaired. Mood ratings can be incorporated into calendar event listings as a helpful adjunct in therapy. Keeping a "concerns" log is a way that staff and family can respond to expressed anxiety: "Let's write that down in our concerns book, so you can talk it over with [therapist]." Such a log accomplishes several aims. The client feels reassured that concerns are "heard," caregivers feel that they are "doing something," and therapists get material that the client might otherwise forget to report.

Many other compensatory aids consist of environmental modifications for safety or convenience. These include such things as using medication dispensers and replacing stoves with timed heaters such as microwaves, toaster ovens, or devices that brew a single cup of hot water or coffee. More elaborate devices for the memory-impaired are computerized reminder systems, telephone reminder services, and electronic wrist bands to signal wandering. Becoming knowledgeable about such devices and services will make the therapist a more valuable resource for the client, caregivers, and treatment team.

Therapists are taught to respect the privacy and confidentiality of therapeutic sessions. With dementing individuals, modifications of strict confidentiality may be necessary. In early stages of the illness, clients are typically still decisionally capable and traditional confidentiality applies. As the individual gradually becomes more impaired, decision making will shift to surrogates. Although no precise principles of confidentiality with the cognitively impaired have yet been developed, the therapist will always convey respect to the impaired person by seeking consent before discussing issues with family members or other caregivers. With increasing impairment, members of the caregiving team become more important as providers of therapeutic care. Therapists should clarify with the client as early as possible the necessity of eventually involving the whole team to provide the best possible care. The client should be encouraged to specify what issues or topics should always remain "off limits" to others, regardless of dementia severity. These measures may involve much needed discussions of lifelong "secrets" such as abortions, affairs, business misadventures, or other events or feelings for which the client wants and deserves absolute confidentiality.

Another related treatment area that arises in therapy with cognitively impaired clients is the potential conflict of interest between serving the client and serving a facility in which the client resides. In home-based therapy as well, the therapist can feel caught between a dementing client and family members. The institutional issues often revolve around the facility's desire to stop a mildly deviant behavior, such as pacing or complaining, which the client seems to enjoy. The family issues may revolve around a decision for placement (e.g., the daughter "instructs" the therapist to get Mom to agree to go to the nursing home). Again, there are currently no widely accepted principles or regulations in this area. A reasonable approach is for the therapist always to assume that the primary responsibility is to the client but to make an effort to work closely and communicate well with facilities and families.

COMMUNICATING WITH THE COGNITIVELY IMPAIRED: VALIDATION

No discussion of psychotherapy with the cognitively impaired would be complete without mention of Naomi Feil and her theory and techniques for communicating with dementing individuals. (Feil, 1993). Feil presents a psychodynamic theoretical interpretation of the apparently random, confused verbalizations and movements of these individuals. In its simplest form, she posits that disturbed, demented persons are attempting to resolve earlier developmental issues in order to die in peace. By "validating" these attempts at resolution, caregivers can aid very disturbed persons in their search for peace. This theory was first posited in contrast to the techniques of "reality orientation," which attempted to reorient the confused individual, either by daily classes or "24-hour" exposure to the correct date, time, names, location, etc. In validation, the caregivers learn to accept and empathize with disoriented older adults rather than to correct them. As an empathetic listener, the caregiver is able to build trust, thus reducing anxiety and improving the client's sense of self-worth and dignity. The techniques embody a strong sense of respect and value for every individual, regardless of dementia severity, idiosyncratic movements or behaviors, levels of emotional agitation, or other characteristics that may cause someone to be dismissed as "just end-stage dementia."

While there is little experimental research based on validation theory, many therapists are enthusiastic about the set of therapeutic techniques Feil brings together for use with dementing individuals. These include the following:

1. Centering before interacting. This is accomplished with 3 minutes of deep breathing by the caregiver, client, or both.
2. Using factual words to build a trust. Don't ask why? but rather who, what, when and where.
3. Rephrasing or paraphrasing. Reflect the person's key words, pitch and tempo of voice; reflect his or her facial expressions.
4. Identifying and using the client's preferred sense. Use visual ("what does it look like?"), auditory ("How does it sound?") or kinesthetic ("Is the pain sharp?") language.
5. Using polarity. Have the individual describe the extreme form of a complaint, such as "What is the worst thing she said to you?"
6. Imagining the opposite. ("Is there ever a time when the man doesn't hide under your bed?")
7. Reminiscing. Explore through past experiences to establish trust and to identify and strengthen coping mechanisms that had been successful in the past.
8. Maintaining close eye contact.
9. Using ambiguity. Substitute ambiguous words (*he, she, it, someone, something*) when reflecting or paraphrasing the client's neologisms (made-up words).
10. Using a clear, low, loving tone of voice.
11. Mirroring. Observe carefully and match or reflect the client's motions and emotions. This is essentially nonverbal paraphrasing.
12. Linking disturbed behavior to an unmet need. Identify when the disturbed behavior is a manifestation of a need for love, usefulness, or emotional expression; help the client satisfy the need.
13. Touching.
14. Using music.

Although Feil draws sharp distinctions between "validation" and insight-oriented psychotherapy, many of her techniques can be regularly and successfully incorporated into the therapeutic relationship. It is likely that these techniques amplify the positive impact of common factors in psychotherapy with the frail elderly in general and specifically in the cognitively impaired. These are also excellent techniques which the therapist can teach to family and staff caregivers. Caregivers frequently find themselves in an oppositional stance toward dementing individuals while attempting to accomplish personal care, transport, or medical care. These techniques help to diffuse the control battles between the caregiver and the dementing person, and build the trust, empathy, and sensitivity, which allow care needs to be met.

Feil originated the validation concepts in a group therapy setting, and the techniques are indeed useful for those who can benefit from group psychotherapy. Group validation concepts include the facilitation of social interaction, opportunities for problem solving, restoration of familiar social roles, and emotional expression.

SUMMARY AND CONCLUSIONS

It is extremely important in any type of group or individual therapy with the cognitively impaired to be clear about the purpose of the group and each individual's goals. In today's medical model, to avoid denial of payment or accusations of fraud, individual and group psychotherapy must be "medically necessary" and the goal of group therapy cannot be socialization. If a therapist incorporates nonverbal techniques into therapy, such as music, movement or art, it must be with a clear understanding of how those techniques are helping a particular client progress to his or her therapeutic goal.

Care models of the future may be less narrowly medical and more able to incorporate both prevention of psychological distress as well as including and interventions that are palliative or growth-oriented, not necessarily curative in nature. A more broadly defined biopsychosocial model would be an ideal framework to deliver the psychotherapeutic services that many persons with cognitive impairment need and deserve.

REFERENCES

Alexopoulos, G. S. (1991). Anxiety and depression in the elderly. *Anxiety in the elderly: Treatment and research* (pp. 63–77). New York: Springer.

American Psychiatric Association. (1994). *Diagnostic and statistical manual of mental disorders* (4th ed.). Washington, DC: Author.

Beck, A. T., Rush, J., Shaw, B., & Emery, G. (1979). *Cognitive therapy of depression.* New York: Guilford.

Burnside, I., & Schmidt, M. G. (Eds.). (1994). *Working with older adults: Group process and techniques.* Boston: Jones and Bartlett.

Camp, C. J., Foss, J. W., Stevens, A. B., Reichard, C. C., McKitrick, L. A., & O'Hanlon, A. M. (1993). Memory training in normal and demented elderly populations: The E-I-E-I-O model. *Experimental Aging Research, 19*(3), 277–290.

Camp, C. J., & McKitrick, L. A. (1992). Memory interventions in Alzheimer's-type dementia populations: Methodological and theoretical issues. In R. L. West & J. D. Sinnott (Eds.), *Everyday memory and aging: Current research and methodology* (pp. 155–172). New York: Springer.

Camp, C. J., & Stevens, A. B. (1990). Spaced-retrieval: A memory intervention for dementia of the Alzheimer's type (DAT). *Clinical Gerontologist, 10,* 58–61.

Cummings, J. L., & Benson, D. F. (1992). *Dementia: A clinical approach* (2nd ed.). Boston: Butterworth.

Evans, D. A., Funkenstein, H. H., & Albert, M. S. (1989). Prevalence of Alzheimer's disease in a community population of older persons. *Journal of the American Medical Association, 262,* 2551–2556.

Feil, N. (1993). *The validation breakthrough: Simple techniques for communicating with people with Alzheimer's-type dementia.* Baltimore, MD: Health Professions Press.

Folstein, M. F., Folstein, S. E., & McHugh, P. R. (1975). "Mini-mental state": A practical method for grading the cognitive state of patients for the clinician. *Journal of Psychiatric Research, 12,* 189–198.

Hausman, C. (1992). Dynamic psychotherapy with elderly demented patients. In G. M. M. Jones & B. M. L. Miesen (Eds.), *Care-giving in dementia* (pp. 181–198). New York: Routledge.

Howard, D. V. (1991). Implicit memory: An expanding picture of cognitive aging. In K. W. Schaie & M. P. Lawton (Eds.), *Annual review of gerontology and geriatrics* (pp 1–22). New York: Springer.

Jones, S. N. (1995). An interpersonal approach to psychotherapy with older persons with dementia. *Professional Psychology: Research and Practice, 26,* 602–607.

Lewinsohn, P. M., Antonuccio, D. O., Steinmetz, J. L., & Teri, L. (1984). *The coping with depression course.* Eugene, OR: Castalia Publishing.

Miesen, B. (1992). Attachment theory and dementia. In G. M. M. Jones & B. M. L. Miesen (Eds.), *Care-giving in dementia* (pp. 38–56). New York: Routledge.

Parmelee, P. A., & Lawton, M. P. (1990). The design of special environments for the aged. In J. E. Birren & K. W. Schaie (Eds.), *The handbook of the psychology of aging* (3rd ed.) (pp. 464–488). New York: Academic Press.

Parmelee, P. A., Katz, I. R., & Lawton, M. P. (1989). Depression among institutionalized aged: Assessment and prevalence estimation. *Journal of Gerontology: Medical Sciences, 44,* M22–M29.

Parmelee, P. A., Katz, I. R., & Lawton, M. P. (1993). Anxiety and its association with depression among institutionalized elderly. *American Journal of Geriatric Psychiatry, 1,* 46–58.

Reisberg, B., Ferris, S. H., & Franssen, E. (1985). An ordinal functional assessment tool for Alzheimer's-type dementia. *Hospital and Community Psychiatry, 36,* 593–595.

Squire, L. R. (1992). Memory and the hippocampus: A synthesis from findings with rats, monkeys, and humans. *Psychological Review, 99,* 195–231.

Storandt, M., & VandenBos, G. R. (1994). *Neuropsychological assessment of dementia and depression in older adults: A clinician's guide.* Washington, DC: American Psychological Association.

Teri, L., & Gallagher-Thompson, D. (1991). Cognitive-behavioral interventions for treatment of depression in Alzheimer's patients. *Gerontologist, 31,* 413–416.

Teri, L., & Logsdon, R. (1991). Identifying pleasant activities for Alzheimer's disease patients: The Pleasant Events Schedule-AD. *The Gerontologist, 31,* 124–127.

Teri, L., & Wagner, A. W. (1992). Alzheimer's disease and depression. *Journal of Consulting and Clinical Psychology, 60,* 379–391.

U.S. Department of Health and Human Services, Office of Inspector General. (May, 1996). *Mental health services in nursing facilities.* New York Regional Office.

Verwoerdt, A. (1981). Individual psychotherapy in senile dementia. In N. E. Miller & G. D. Cohen (Eds.), *Clinical aspects of Alzheimer's disease and senile dementia* (pp. 187–208). New York: Raven Press.

Zarit, S. H., & Zarit, J. M. (1982). Families under stress: Interventions for caregivers of senile dementia patients. *Psychotherapy: Theory, Research and Practice, 19,* 461–471.

5

Emotion in People with Dementia: A Way of Comprehending Their Preferences and Aversions

M. Powell Lawton, Kimberly Van Haitsma, and Margaret Perkinson

In this chapter we argue that people with dementing illness have feelings that, as with people of any age and any state of health, may reveal their likes and dislikes and give cues to their significant others about how best to contribute to a satisfying milieu. We first suggest how emotion fits into the larger picture of quality of life. We then discuss emotion as a behavior that caregivers can be taught to observe and utilize in the care of older patients with dementia. The central section of this chapter consists of a manual for observing emotion and utilizing it in the everyday care of people with dementia.

A VIEW OF QUALITY OF LIFE

Although this report focuses only on the affective aspect of quality of life (QOL) in one limited group, it is useful to anchor QOL among related concepts (see Lawton, 1991, for an extended discussion of

QOL in general). First, a definition of QOL is "the multidimensional evaluation, by both intrapersonal and social-normative criteria, of the person-environment system of an individual in time past, current, and anticipated" (Lawton, 1991, p. 6). The social-normative view of QOL sees the quality of the environment of the person as a clear element in such quality. For the institutionalized person with dementing illness, this "objective" aspect of QOL might be indicated by a high staff-patient ratio, an in-service training program that emphasizes sensitivity and individual care, or a care unit whose architectural design was homelike or that fostered social interaction. We do not suggest that every resident will benefit from such features. We simply suggest that, on the average, more people will benefit if exposed to these environmental features than if not exposed. This is the *objective* view of QOL, exemplified in setting standards for care and care environments because we think they will improve the average well-being of residents.

If we turn to the individual rather than the context in which the individual lives, we can identify another sector of QOL that also may be characterized as objective: the person's behavior, evaluated in terms of its "competence" or adaptive quality. We are used to thinking of a child's school performance, a worker's efficiency as judged by a supervisor, or a person's social skill as indicators of generalized competence in living. Among people with dementing illness, many such benchmarks are familiar: intellectual ability, activities of daily living skill, the absence of agitated, disturbed, or socially inappropriate behaviors, and so on. They are characterized as an aspect of QOL because, in general, the more such behaviors are performed according to socially prescribed standards, the more likely a person's goals in life are to be attainable.

Still focusing on the individual brings us to the *subjective* aspects of QOL. This is the realm where we depend on the person's own view. We allow for the fact that two people may be in the same objective situation—let us say, married, with equal incomes—but may have radically differing evaluations of their situation. One person considers herself happily married, the other is unhappily married. One considers family income adequate, the other inadequate, and so on. Thus, we must take account of how each individual perceives the important domains of everyday life, such as family, work, leisure time, or housing. On a more generalized level, people differ greatly in their overall happiness, mental health, or generalized psychological well-being. It is extremely difficult for another person to view the "inside" of the person who is evaluating her own life. Although judgments of our own QOL take account of the objective quality of our external situation, at least as important is the emotional quality of each of these domains of everyday life and our subjective evaluation of life as a whole. But both the objective and subjective definitions of QOL are necessary to comprehend how well off the person is. Further, the relationship between objective and subjective indicators is important to know and, therefore, to investigate.

QUALITY OF LIFE IN DEMENTIA

If we accept the above view that QOL must be assessed in the sectors of environmental quality, behavior competence, domains of everyday life, and life as a whole, how can this framework be applied to people with dementing illness? Examples have been given earlier of environmental and behavioral indicators of QOL (see also more complete discussion of QOL in Alzheimer's disease in Burgener & Chiverton, 1992, and Lawton, 1994, as well as a systematic literature search and critical review by Howard & Rockwood, 1995). In the subjective realm we run into great difficulty, however. Notably absent from the large body of work examining dementing illness are efforts to understand the feelings and preferences of the patients themselves (Cotrell & Schulz, 1993; Herskovitz, 1995). Researchers have tended to dismiss the possibility of gaining useful information about the experience of dementia via self-report. Rather, as Herskovitz (1995) asserts, "very little is being asked of those with dementia; much is speculated and asserted about them" (p. 148). Reasons for the neglect of the patient's perspective include the pervasive stereotype that dementia patients are lacking in selfhood, professionals' limited understanding of the concept of self-awareness, their failure to consider premorbid styles of self-expression, and methodological difficulties in assessment.

Recent analyses of people with dementia have suggested that a loss of self or a process of "unbecoming" are ascribed to this illness by many clinicians. However, many studies fail to consider and assess the wide variation in levels of self-awareness across both persons and areas of functioning. That is, there may be extensive individual differences not only in overall level of self-awareness but also in the specific patterns of unawareness across functional areas as well as different types of awareness (Danner & Friesen, 1996). To the degree that those with dementia retain awareness of their deficits across a range of functions, their ability to report on their emotional reactions to their deficits might be preserved.

Neglect of the patient perspective in dementia may also reflect the failure to consider premorbid expressive styles when drawing conclusions about a person's internal experience (Cotrell & Schulz, 1993; Danner & Friesen, 1996). An understanding of premorbid expressive style can help to bring order and meaning to the apparently random expressions of the demented patient. What appears to be indiscriminate, meaningless emotional behavior might instead represent a distorted attempt to communicate one's feelings and needs to caregivers. The new wave in attempting to understand the subjectivity of dementing illness asserts that the person with dementia clearly has feelings but lacks the ability to express them in some of the usual ways.

Informed by the knowledge that the demented person has a long-standing tendency to react strongly and negatively to particular circumstances, caregivers and researchers might be able to interpret better their signals of emotional distress. A consideration of these challenges in translating the demented person's message reveals the vital role of careful assessment in understanding their self-reported inner experience.

The need to translate dementia patients' oftentimes distorted communication constitutes one of several methodological obstacles to accurate interpretation of self-report information. The ability to "read" a patient is facilitated by assessment efforts that emphasize attention to complementary sources of information, including verbal, facial, postural, vocal, and contextual cues, as well as by the establishment of rapport, which serves to allay patients' fears and mistrust, thereby minimizing emotional barriers to self-revelation (Cotrell & Schulz, 1993). Further, given the extreme fluctuations in dementia patients' levels of lucidity or self-awareness, the usefulness of self-report information might be maximized by making every effort to interview a patient at what is a "good time" for him or her (Cotrell & Schulz, 1993).

A final methodological obstacle to obtaining useful self-report information from dementia patients might be the method by which the data are sought. For example, studies in which dementia patients are asked to reminisce about past emotional experiences (Danner & Friesen, 1996) might overtax their limited memory capabilities (Cotrell & Schulz, 1993). Some researchers have attenuated these limitations by gathering historical data by proxy (e.g., from family members) to use in cuing the patient (e.g., Danner & Friesen, p. 5) or by attending to nonverbal indicators of emotion to use as probes for the patient's "here and now" emotional experience (Cotrell & Schulz, 1993). "The degree and nature of impairments may prevent the individual from providing an objective historical account of symptoms, yet still allow an accurate report of the individual's current experience of the disease" (Cotrell & Schulz, 1993, p. 209).

In summary, it requires considerable cognitive and social skill to observe one's own state, compare it to internal and social standards regarding what is desirable, assess the feelings associated with the state, and report such evaluations to an outsider, as we do in response to a question like "How are things today?" The person with dementing illness is typically severely limited in observational, conceptual, and reporting ability. The focal problem with which this report is concerned is thus how to discern the subjective QOL of patients who are limited in their ability to introspect and report their QOL evaluations.

WHY IS IT USEFUL TO KNOW THE QUALITY OF THE EMOTIONAL LIFE OF PEOPLE WITH DEMENTIA?

We have already implied one reason for wishing to comprehend the emotions being experienced by the person with dementing illness. The first is a value-based reason. Dementia patients have the same right that all people have to maximize positive feelings and minimize negative feelings. Simply being able to recognize that they experience good and bad moments will do much to enable caregiving staff and families to respond to the individuality and humanity of the patient with Alzheimer's disease. "The Alzheimer patient is still a person with a past, a present, and a future" is the first lesson caregivers should learn.

The second reason follows from the first. Granting the patient a personality, it follows logically that he or she has likes and dislikes and is capable of communicating them somehow. Our major assertion for this chapter is that even when cognitive and verbal communicative capacity are greatly reduced, the ability to display preferences and aversions may persist. In many ways, the emotions represent a developmentally early system of both responding to and controlling one's external environment. This suggests that emotion may also be later to disappear from the repertory of communication skills than more verbally dependent functions. In the next sections, a few general comments about emotion are offered; these are followed by a brief summary of recent research on emotion in dementia.

The Nature of Emotion

Emotion is evidenced at neurological, neurophysiological, behavioral, and subjective levels. All are important and all are frequently simultaneous in their activity during emotion. We sometimes mistakenly assume that emotion consists only of a subjectively recognized feeling. Although all levels of emotional experience are important, it may simply be noted that the face has been repeatedly validated as one indicator of emotion, even across nations and cultures (Ekman, Friesen, O'Sullivan, & Chen, 1987). Specifically, unique patterns of facial musculature have been demonstrated for specific emotions such as joy, anger, disgust, and others (Ekman & Friesen, 1978). Voice quality (Caporael, Lukaszewski, & Culbertson, 1983) and body position and movement (DeLong, 1970) similarly afford clues to people's emotional states.

Emotion in Dementia

A more complete review of research on emotion in dementia may be found in Shue, Beck, and Lawton (1996). Suffice it to note here that most research has documented the continued operation of both receptive and communicative emotion among people with dementia (Albert, Cohen, & Koff, 1991; Allender & Kaszniak, 1989; Danner & Friesen, 1996; Hurley, Volicer, Hanrahan, Honde, & Volicer, 1992;

Tappen & Barry, 1995). The present authors' research is described in greater detail because this research used the instrument on which this chapter is focused.

The Apparent Affect Rating Scale (AARS; Lawton, Van Haitsma, & Klapper, 1996) was designed as an observational tool for a research project in which moderate to moderately–severely demented nursing home residents were subjects (one of a set of 10 cooperative research projects funded by the National Institute on Aging to study special care units; Ory, 1994). The AARS entails rating three negative emotions (anger, anxiety/fear, and depression/sadness) and two positive emotions (pleasure and interest) over a 5-minute period (unless another time frame is specified, such as 2 weeks for related methods such as emotion questionnaires developed for family or activity therapist use; Lawton et al., 1996). The rater is asked to indicate the amount of time he or she observed a target resident displaying each of the emotions: never, less than 16 seconds, 16 to 59 seconds, 1 to 2 minutes, or over 2 minutes. Raters are given signs or indicators of each of the emotions, such as clenched teeth, grimace, shouting, etc., as indicators of anger. The AARS as used in this form is depicted in Table 5.1.

In our research, we began by testing the reliability and the validity of the AARS. Reliability of raters represents the extent to which two raters observing the same behavior could agree on (1) which emotion was being expressed, if any, and (2) how long it lasted. Two trained research assistants agreed very well (Lawton et al., 1996), within limits. Although anger and sadness were very infrequent, when they did occur, two observers agreed (kappas ranged from .78 to .89). Reliability was also tested for other methods and other types of rater, with less good results (Lawton et al., 1997). These issues are discussed later in this chapter.

Validity was tested by determining the correlations between AARS ratings and measures of emotion-related attributes obtained from totally independent sources (Lawton et al., 1996). The general outcome was that AARS scores correlated significantly with other measures of similar attributes, although the sizes of the correlations were modest. Some examples include a correlation between AARS Sadness and the Multidimensional Observation Scale for Elderly Subjects (MOSES; Helmes et al., 1987) depression scale of .25; AARS Anxiety and the Cohen-Mansfield Agitation Index (Cohen-Mansfield,

TABLE 5.1 Apparent Affect Rating Scale

RESIDENT'S NAME: _____ UNIT: _____

OBSERVER'S NAME: _____ DATE: _____ TIME:_____

Please rate the extent or duration of each affect over a 5-minute observation period. Some possible signs of each emotion are listed. If you see *no sign* of a particular feeling, rate "Never." Use "Can't tell" only when you are really uncertain.

	9	1	2	3	4	5
	Can't tell	Never	< 16 sec	16–59 sec	1–2 min	2 min

PLEASURE
Signs: Smile, laugh, stroking, touching with "approach" manner, nodding, singing, arm or hand outreach, open-arm gesture.

ANGER
Signs: Clenched teeth, grimace, shout, yell, curse, berate, push, physical aggression or implied aggression such as fist shaking, pursed lips, eyes narrowed, knit brow.

ANXIETY/FEAR
Signs: Furrowed brow, motoric restlessness, repeated or agitated motion, facial expression of fear or worry, withdrawal from other, tremor, tight facial muscles, calls repetitively, hand wringing, leg jiggling, eyes wide.

DEPRESSION/SADNESS
Signs: Cry, tears, moan, sigh, mouth turned down at corners, eyes/head turned down and face expressionless, wiping eyes.

INTEREST
Signs: Eyes following object, intent fixation on object or person, visual scanning, facial, motoric, or verbal feedback to other, eye contact maintained, body or vocal response to music, turn body or move toward person or object.

Marks, & Rosenthal, 1989) of .32; AARS Pleasure and Activity Therapists' Sociability ratings, correlation of .44; AARS Interest and Mattis
(1976) Dementia Rating Scale, correlation of .22. Another type of
validity was demonstrated when we examined how the AARS varied
across four experimentally chosen contexts (Lawton et al., 1997):
Morning care, mealtime, "down time," and activity-therapy time.
Interest was least frequent and the absence of affect was the most
often observed state during down time (i.e., no regular activity or
scheduled routine). Pleasure was most prevalent in the activity context. Anxiety was most prevalent during morning care.

It thus seems adequately demonstrated that the AARS is able to
capture observable states in cognitively impaired institutionalized
elders in such a way that there is both consensus among observers
and internal consistency in the way these observed emotions are
related to emotions and contexts measured in totally different ways.

USING EMOTION IN DEMENTIA CARE

This positive conclusion brings us back to the uses of observed
emotion in dementia. Even if we can "read" the feelings being displayed by the patient, of what use is that ability? We suggested earlier
that this skill could be useful in providing care. Knowing what a
person likes or dislikes is what guides a great deal of normal social
interchange. When in doubt, we ask questions like "Do you want to
go to the movies or take a walk?" When the person with dementia
does not articulate preferences verbally, it is easy to ignore his or
her wishes. Perhaps the best-known exception to this practice is the
anger or anxiety that is so often expressed when the patient's body
space is invaded by the nursing assistant during the performance
of personal care. Pacing, shouting, and repetitive movements are
recognized as signs of agitation. These are only a few of the many
possible signals sent by cognitively impaired people that are potentially useful in planning positive care. A smile is a sure sign of pleasure, but how many of us routinely register a short step taken toward
us by the patient as a sign of pleasurable approach or the relaxation
of jaw muscles as pleasure? If we knew this language better we would
be much more adept in the small aspects of everyday care. Can
we discriminate the food preferences of a patient through such

observation? If we have to change her position, is one position more comfortable than another? Can television, radio, or recorded music be programmed according to the patient's taste? Choice of clothing? Is one programmed activity a delight to the resident and another disliked or not viewed as relevant? Topics for conversation? One staff member or another? This list is open-ended and very long. We suggest that beyond what the impaired person can tell you, the subtle facial and nonverbal behaviors give us clues about many small—and sometimes very significant—features of life that define everyday quality of life for such people.

Another important rationale for learning how to read patients' feelings is the way they affect the caregiver. Whether the caregiver is a therapist, a certified nursing assistant, or a family member, his or her morale depends strongly on maintaining a sense of accomplishment or an ongoing demonstration that the effects of one's efforts have an impact on patient well-being. Sensitivity to these signals from the care receiver provides highly reinforcing feedback. The caregiver's behavior can thus become shaped to grow progressively in the direction of giving the care receiver more rewards and fewer punishments, with correspondingly increased caregiver morale.

The rationale for utilizing this particular route to the interior of the dementia patient's mind thus seems compelling enough to warrant the introduction of training in reading emotion to the preparation of caregiving professionals, family members, and volunteers. The amount of training required varies strongly with the background of the people being trained and the purpose of the observation of emotion.

The research assistants whose work was reported earlier in this chapter received about 40 hours of training, with frequent booster training (Lawton et al., 1996). In a later research project we attempted "minimalist" training of certified nursing assistants (CNAs) to perform this same task (Lawton et al., 1997). This training consisted of a 30-minute small-group training session, followed by four practice sessions where a single CNA and a single researcher observed the same subject and performed estimated-time ratings (as in Table 5.1) independently. Agreement was poor. For the next project, Van Haitsma and her staff (personal communication) increased the amount of training time and used only CNAs who were prechosen for their judged observational skill. Their reliability improved but was still far below that achieved by researchers. Minimal training also proved ineffective for family members.

We thus conclude that there is no shortcut to achieving skill in noticing and rating the observed behaviors that display the emotion states of the demented patient. What has not yet been done is to embed training in rating emotion into professional in-service training in such a way that learning occurs over a period of time, rather than being expected to occur in a single or short-term training session. All caregivers require periodic training but, most importantly, they should engage in repeated practice sessions with feedback from someone already trained in this skill.

OBSERVING AND RATING EMOTION IN DEMENTIA: A CAREGIVER'S MANUAL

As an aid to training to observe and rate affect, the remainder of this chapter is devoted to a first manual for observing emotion in dementia. We suggest that the place to begin training caregiving staff for observing emotion in everyday clinical care is first to provide training in the formal process of using the AARS. Following the attainment of proficiency in using the formal AARS Rating system, the skills involved in noticing and classifying the emotion are likely to be in place. From that point on, observing emotion during clinical care can be accomplished in informal fashion. The focal task thereafter becomes one of using the information on emotion displays by people with dementia during care, treatment, or programming. Our research team has also produced a 20-minute videotape, "Recognizing Emotion in Persons with Dementia," produced by Rayburn and Rusk and distributed by Terra Nova Films. The tape provides a rationale for how clinical staff can use this source of information, together with a number of examples of facial expressions of people with dementia.

Even if we know that Alzheimer's disease patients experience sad, happy, and other types of emotions, their cognitive impairment stands out so strongly that it is easy to ignore their mood states. In mild and moderately severe states, some Alzheimer patients can both recognize their own feelings, however, and verbalize them to others.

Some patients are totally unable to introspect about their feelings, and it is likely that beyond some point of cognitive impairment, this is no longer possible for anyone. Therefore, it is likely that the emotions of many Alzheimer's patients can be determined only by observation.

What's wrong with observation as a method is that (1) we are not used to depending only on observation and therefore we may not have practiced reading the emotional meaning of facial and motor expressions and (2) trying to judge what is inside another person gives full rein to "projecting" or "reading in" what is in the observer's mind more than what is in the patient's mind. Our approach is based on the conviction that

- The signs of emotions can be read in the observable nonverbal behaviors of people.
- These signs can be learned.
- Practice in observation can make most of us into reliable observers of Alzheimer patients' emotional states.

Where to Look for Emotion

1.   *The face* is the most obvious place—we are all used to looking at another person's face for signs of how he or she is feeling or signs of their response to us.

2.   *The voice*—the loudness or softness, the pitch, the speed of words, the emphasis on particular words, the degree to which expostulation or sudden changes in voice quality appear—all of these can be signs of emotion.

3.   *The body*—"body language" is familiar to us as an unconscious way in which people give expression to their feelings and wishes. This includes the way a person walks, sits, or stands, the gestures she or he makes with arms, hands, or fingers. It also includes the speed, rhythm, or jerkiness of movements. It includes the way positions or movements occur in relation to other people, such as directly facing, slightly averted, moving toward, moving away, and so on.

4.   *The eyes* are a special case of both facial expression and body movement and can be considered only one element in these settings. "Eye contact" stands on its own as worthy of indicating an external

object on which the person's attention is focused. Eye contact, gaze, and focused observation can, with practice, be distinguished from random eye movement or the "blank stare."

5.   *Touch* (usually with fingers) is another special case worthy of mention because it usually means an approach, often liking, whether of another person or an object. Touching or rubbing an object or surface may also be either a search for sensory enjoyment alone or for exploration (interest in something outside the self).

The Basic Emotions: Positive and Negative (Like and Dislike)

There is something special about the seemingly oversimplified distinction between positive and negative emotion. These are, in fact, the most basic emotions that are recognizable in newborn infants. We never cease in our gut reactions to *like* or *dislike* something, which is the most usual form in which positive and negative emotion appears.

The like-dislike distinction is very relevant to programming and care for Alzheimer's patients. But since they often cannot tell us what they like and dislike, it is up to us to try to read their likes and dislikes. Fortunately, we get reasonably good clues from behavior about the gross positive-negative distinction.

It should be evident that there is also a neutral category, a big one. The fact is, most of the time most people are not showing either positive or negative signs of emotion, disliking, or liking. A lot of everyday life for the Alzheimer's patient is also likely to be emotionally neutral. The absence of emotion is harder to define than the presence of emotion. But definitely in the neutral category are simple lack of engagement, obliviousness to what is going on, drowsiness. Repetitive pathological behavior such as agitation, pacing, or shouting, on the other hand, is more likely than not to be a sign of anxiety (negative emotion) unless clear signs to the contrary are exhibited (e.g., a wanderer who shows by a grin or other approach behavior that this is an enjoyable task). A general state of relaxation and contentment is, in contrast, frequently a positive and liked state—but distinguishing this from drowsiness, withdrawal, or simple absence of engagement can be difficult.

Here are some indicators of the five states most important to recognize:

Pleasure

Smile

Laugh

Stroke

Touching other with "approach" manner

Nodding

Singing

Crinkling of eyes

Wide eyes

Raised eyebrows

Turn body toward something

Open-arm gesture

Anxiety

Furrowed brow with drooping lower face

Motoric restlessness

Rocking and other repetitious motions

Sigh

Withdraw from other without anger

Tremor

Hand-wringing

Pacing

Moaning, whining, or high-pitched crying

Repetitive calling

Hunched shoulders

Strained, inflexible body position

Rapid, noisy, or irregular breathing

Anger

Clenched teeth

Grimace

Shout

Curse

Berate

Push

Physical aggression

Move aggressively toward another

Move away from other with signs of anger

Tight face

Furrowed brow with other anger signs

Lower jaw out

Lips pursed, downward curve

Sadness or Depression

Tears

Moans

Eyebrows slant downward at corners, with or without furrowed brow

Mouth and other face muscles droop

Lower lip hangs down

Corners of mouth downward

Eyes directed downward

Slumped shoulders

"Empty looking" eyes

Interest or "Engagement"

Eyes follow objects

Intent gaze on object or person

Scans the environment with head, eye, or body movement

Facial, muscular or verbal response to other

Eye contact maintained

Body or vocal response to music

Moving toward a person or object

Wide open eyes

Gaze moves across a wide angle, with head and eye movement

Focus on a motor task, such as dressing, eating, walking, etc.

Social interaction

Participation in an activity

The Apparent Affect Rating Scale

Now look at the Apparent Affect Rating Scale (AARS, Table 5.1). You will see brief written examples of each of the two positive (pleasure and interest) and three negative (anger, anxiety, sadness) emotions. Your job is to watch the person for 5 minutes, then stop and rate these five emotions. On the right hand side are columns that allow you to estimate whether an emotion was observed and, if so, during approximately how much of the 5 minutes of observation you saw this emotion being displayed. It may never have occurred (column 1: Never). If it occurred at all, do your best to estimate how long the emotion was actually visible during the 5-minute period. Some emotions may be visible only for a split-second, while others may go on a long time. It may well be that no emotion at all occurs over 5 minutes, in which case all would be marked "1: Never." Use "9: Can't tell" only when (1) you could not see the person or the observation time was less than 5 minutes or (2) when some emotion *may* have occurred but you are not sure. After each 5-minute period, you should have one check for each emotion.

Observational Procedure

Positioning for Observations. It is necessary to decide where to stand or sit in order to observe the patient. A clear and unobtrusive view is necessary for an observation.

Area of Observation. The area where the observation takes place directly affects the distance from observer to subject. It is possible to be placed anywhere from 8 to 25 feet away from a subject as long as a clear view of the face is maintained. However, if the areas of observation are small rooms, or if the observation takes place in a bedroom, it may be necessary to observe a subject at a closer distance.

Context of Observation. The first priority of observation is to get a clear view of the subject's face, since the face generally holds the most expression of emotion. In most cases it is also helpful to have a view of the subject's hands and feet. Observing the total body can be helpful in identifying anxiety (wringing hands), or pleasure (clapping hands, tapping feet); this may be especially true in the case of activity observations. However, if a subject is asleep during an observation, it obviously is not as essential to see the total body or stand at such a far distance. In certain situations, it is also helpful to be close enough to a subject in order to hear any conversation or noise between subjects, since these signs may indicate emotions which are not indicated by facial expression.

Resident to Be Observed. Because Alzheimer's patients have varying levels of cognitive functioning, it is important to keep in mind the individuality of each subject. In general, distance from researcher to subject is not a crucial factor for those who are severely demented or have high levels of cognitive impairment, primarily because the presence of the observer may not be noticed and therefore may not be obtrusive. Subjects who are mildly demented present more of a challenge. The observer must be careful to be far enough away so as to not be "noticed" by the subject. Eye contact in particular often results in the resident's attempting to engage the observer. In general, it is best to keep in mind that discretion is more important than distance from the subject in doing naturalistic observation.

Subject Reactivity

Frequently, residents will approach the observer either to chat or inquire about the observer's purpose. There are a few different scenarios that can occur, but the following three occur most frequently. First, it is very important to avoid eye contact with the subject being observed. If the subject does approach the observer, the observer should either avoid the interaction by ignoring the subject or acknowledge the subject by saying "I'm in the middle of working right now. I'll talk with you in about 5 minutes." Second, there is the possibility of being approached by a person other than the one being observed. The same techniques as above should be employed in this situation as well. Finally, residents who ask for help during the observation should be told, "I have to do some work right now. I can help you in about 5 minutes." In general, residents get used to the presence of an observer with a watch and clipboard fairly quickly. Resident reactivity thus decreases over time, even among those with only mild impairment.

SOME PROBLEM AREAS IN OBSERVING AFFECT

How Cognitive Impairment Can Mask Emotion

A first fact to be aware of is that cognitive impairment makes people unable to understand and process some of what goes on in their environment. They may appear unreactive or they may miss the signals that come from other people. The Alzheimer's patient may appear preoccupied, withdrawn, or otherwise "out of it." Thus, a first task is to understand that withdrawal and the loss of some earlier-life abilities and personality traits is not to be confused with the absence of emotion.

Baseline of Apparent Affect

The rating of apparent affect is a complex task. The human observer interprets observed behavior and emotion, at least in part, based on what is considered to be a "baseline," or normal level, of emotion for the individual they are observing. The observer develops a sense of what is normal for a given individual over the course of the usually extended period of observation. For example, a demented individual may engage in repetitive movement as a matter of course throughout the day. This behavior in and of itself may not represent anxiety for this person. However, after observing the individual for a while (including the training period), the observer develops a sense of changes in the intensity or rhythm of movements and signals that *do* denote the onset of anxiety for that person. Obviously the "baseline" of apparent affect will be different for each person observed.

Physical Impairment

Part of rating apparent affect includes at least some knowledge of a person's physical impairments. Many disease processes or even aging alone can produce changes in facial expression and/or body movement. For example, Parkinson's disease can produce a characteristically "flat affect" facial expression and tremulousness when an individual is attempting to move. Cerebrovascular accidents can lead to a drooping of half of the face and paralysis of an arm or leg. Tardive dyskinesia can produce strange mouth, tongue, and body movements. Chronic obstructive pulmonary disease in severe cases can produce shortness of breath and wheezing even with limited movement. Resting tremors in the hands are very common in many neurological conditions. Impairments in vision or hearing may reinforce an impression of unreactivity. Wrinkles may give an impression of permanent anger, worry or mirth, if the observer has no previous knowledge of how *changes* in expression occur. Knowledge of these conditions should be used to help interpret apparent affect and inform the human observer about the relative usefulness of its cues.

Apparent affect is usually thought of in terms of a state the individual is experiencing at the moment, one that comes and goes depending on a variety of internal and external situations. However, difficulties arise when one is confronted with individuals who appear to have an emotional state etched permanently into their face and body. Is this depression or the result of many years of simple aging or of a disease process loosening the elasticity of the facial skin, osteoporosis of the spine, and osteoarthritis in the joints? This gets us back to the importance of having a sense of the baseline of apparent affect for a given individual. Minute movements of the face and changes in intensity of expression become crucial in rating an individual's apparent affect.

Distinguishing Between Interest and No Affect

Is the person actually mentally engaged in (or, attending to) some aspect of his or her environment, as opposed to being merely physically present? If a person is not sleeping and is not exhibiting null behavior or a fixed gaze, he or she is probably demonstrating interest. The difficulty then lies in the judgment as to whether a person's gaze on an object or person is "intent" as opposed to simply random or fixed. Fortunately, few things in the environment are totally static; thus, if a person is demonstrating interest, it is highly likely that his or her gaze will shift periodically, as in the criterion, "eyes follow object." Because a rating of "no affect" requires that a person demonstrate no movement in his or her eyes, face, or body, interest would be coded when a person's gaze follows something in the environment. When the subject is engaged in any focused activity such as eating, calling out, or even in the repetitive or pathological movements but no other emotion is evident, interest is assumed to be present.

The Relationship Between Interest and Other Affects

Early in their training our researchers showed a tendency to assume that the presence of sadness, anxiety, anger, or pleasure automatically signaled the presence of interest. It does, in fact. But we gain nothing from such double coding. Therefore our rule is that if any of those other four affects are coded, interest is not. Interest therefore stands for interest by itself only when some other feeling state is not coded. In other words, pleasure, anxiety, anger, and sadness take precedence over interest.

Distinguishing Between No Affect and Depression

Because severe depression may be characterized by flat affect, and by "eyes/head downturned and face expressionless," it may be difficult to differentiate depression from no affect. However, since no affect is further characterized by a lack of movement of the eyes, face, and body, then, if movement accompanies a blank expression, depression would be coded. Depression is the most difficult affect to recognize. Because it is difficult to recognize, it is probably often missed by researchers, care staff, and family members. Clinically depressed people would be identified by professional staff and be included as subjects in training people to use the AARS. In such people, it is likely that ambiguous signs such as those noted above may in fact be signs of depression. This, in turn, gives raters a basis for comparing such signs in other people.

"Hot" vs. "Cold" Affects

Affects differ in the speed of their expression and duration. For example, anger and pleasure tend to be expressed as "flashes" of emotion. Their expression is often fleeting and easily missed if the human observer is not attentive. In contrast, interest and anxiety, and often depression, tend to be expressed for longer periods of time and are more apparent to the observer.

TRAINING STAFF TO USE THE AARS

A classroom-style introduction to the AARS, based on the material in this chapter and on the videotape, if available, is the best beginning for staff of any discipline to learn to recognize emotion. After the introductory classroom and videotape discussion, each person should be given recording forms and assigned a quota of 5-minute observations to do on their own, intermixed with daily clinical duties. Following these solitary practice ratings, a second group discussion should be scheduled within a week (embedded in a class or meeting with other purposes if necessary). This is purely a feedback session, where people can discuss their experiences in making their first ratings and bring up problems and ambiguities.

The third element in training may be the most difficult to accomplish, but it is also the most essential: A series of two-observer reliability ratings. If there is time in the training schedule, pairs of two types could be formed: experienced rater and novice rater, or two novice raters. For either type the two raters begin together, watching from the same vantage point but recording independently without looking at what the other rater writes. At the end of a single 5-minute period, the raters should then go to a quiet location and immediately compare their ratings. Where they disagree, they can discuss and sometimes resolve disagreements. It is desirable to train each person with several different partners in the reliability testing process.

We suggest that such reliability trials be spread over about 2 weeks, with four to five observations done each week by each observer. The staff member's training to a minimum level would be complete at this point. If the trainer has the time and the services of someone with enough statistical knowledge to calculate correlation coefficients, displaying them by pairs of raters is an instructive procedure.

Such formal training is indispensable in teaching direct-care staff how to observe emotion clinically. After learning to use the AARS in a formal way, the staff person will always observe people in a new way. Even without trying, she or he will note the unmistakable signs of different emotions in everyday care situations. The usefulness of this new skill is greatly enhanced, however, by building in emotion observation as a routine aspect of a care planning team's discussions. Only in this way can one good observer communicate to colleagues knowledge useful to all team members. The ultimate purpose of observing emotion is to relate the emotion to the everyday events that constitute care, treatment, and enriching activity programs. The care planning team ought to incorporate the routine reporting of the prevalence of the different emotions and the conditions that are associated with both positive and negative feelings. The care planning written record should include details such as observations about what types of care and activities have been observed to please or displease the resident. One use of records is the possibility of using them to map change over time or in response to new programs. Inservice training within a single discipline should incorporate affect observation training in order to increase the ability of a professional to assess whether the care being given at a given moment is being received well.

Finally, ongoing in-service training in using emotional cues for treatment purposes would ensure higher-quality observation of emotion if a set of formal two-person reliabilities were repeated periodically, perhaps twice a year. What researchers call "rater drift" occurs as trained people perform many ratings in a routine manner and develop their own internal and sometimes incorrect standards for how to rate. This drift is an unconscious process, and raters are always surprised when shown the extent to which they begin to deviate from one another and from the standard procedures over time. The same drift happens, of course, when the observation is purely qualitative and clinical. The formal repeat-reliability testing is simply a means for displaying to staff how to correct for drift.

CONCLUSION

Good care for people with dementia requires a continuing search for means by which caregivers may comprehend the needs of such people and build this understanding into the way they give care. The emotional states of dementia patients are a neglected source of such cues. We have reviewed the place of the emotions in well-being, the reasons for looking toward observed emotion as an aid in clinical care, and research data attesting to the ability of trained people to "read" such subjective states. Training to use observed emotion requires extended instruction and practice. We have described procedures through which direct-care staff may be introduced to these procedures. If successful, these skills have hope for leading caregivers to the preferences and aversions of people with dementia and to the ability to shape their own caregiving effort through recognition of the recipients' responses to their clinical care.

REFERENCES

Albert, M. S., Cohen, C., & Koff, E. (1991). Perception of affect in patients with dementia of the Alzheimer type. *Archives of Neurology, 48,* 791–795.

Allender, J., & Kaszniak, A. W. (1989). Processing of emotional cues in patients with dementia of the Alzheimer's type. *International Journal of Neurosciences, 46,* 147–155.

Burgener, S. C., & Chiverton, P. (1992). Conceptualizing psychological well-being in cognitively impaired older persons. *Image, 24,* 209–214.

Caporael, L. R., Lukaszewski, M. P., & Culbertson, G. H. (1983). Secondary baby talk: Judgments by institutionalized elderly and their caregivers. *Journal of Personality and Social Psychology, 44,* 746–754.

Cohen-Mansfield, J., Marx, M. S., & Rosenthal, A. S. (1989). A description of agitation in a nursing home. *Journal of Gerontology: Medical Sciences, 44,* M77–M84.

Cotrell, V., & Schulz, R. (1993). The perspective of the patient with Alzheimer's disease. *The Gerontologist, 33,* 205–211.

Danner, D. D., & Friesen, W. V. (1996). Are severely impaired Alzheimer' patients aware of their environment and illness? *Journal of Clinical Geropsychology, 2,* 321–335.

DeLong, A. J. (1970). The microspatial structure of the older person. In L. A. Pastalan & D. H. Carson (Eds.), *Spatial behavior of older people* (pp. 68–87). Ann Arbor: University of Michigan Institute of Gerontology.

Ekman, P., & Friesen, W. V. (1978). *Facial action coding system.* Palo Alto CA: Consulting Psychologists Press.

Ekman, P., Friesen, W. P., O'Sullivan, M., & Chan, A. (1987). Universals and cultural differences in the judgments of facial expressions of emotion. *Journal of Personality and Social Psychology, 53,* 712–717.

Helmes, E., Csapo, K. G., & Short, J. A. (1987). Standardization and validation of the Multidimensional Observation Scale for Elderly Subjects (MOSES). *Journal of Gerontology, 42,* 395–405.

Herskovitz, E. (1995). Struggling over subjectivity: Debates about the "self" and Alzheimer's disease. *Medical Anthropology Quarterly, 9,* 146–164.

Howard, K., & Rockwood, K. (1995). Quality of life in Alzheimer's disease. *Dementia, 6,* 113–116.

Hurley, A. C., Volicer, B., Hanrahan, P. A., Houde, S., & Volicer, L. (1992). Assessment of discomfort in advanced Alzheimer patients. *Research in Nursing and Health, 15,* 369–377.

Lawton, M. P. (1991). A multidimensional view of quality of life in frail elders. In J. E. Birren, J. Lubben, J. C. Rowe, & D. E. Deutchman (Eds.), *The concept and measurement of quality of life* (pp. 3–27). New York: Academic Press.

Lawton, M. P. (1994). Quality of life in Alzheimer's disease. *Alzheimer's Disease and Related Disorders, 29,* Supplement 138–150.

Lawton, M. P., Perkinson, M., Van Haitsma, K., Ruckdeschel, K., Corn, J., Seddon, K., & Clunk, L. (1997). *Emotion in dementia: Its measurement and comprehension by caregivers.* Final report on Grant TRG 90-001 from the Alzheimer's Association. Philadelphia Geriatric Center.

Lawton, M. P., Van Haitsma, K., & Klapper, J. (1996). Observed affect in nursing home residents with Alzheimer's disease. *Journal of Gerontology: Psychological Sciences, 51B,* P3–P14.

Mattis, S. (1976). Mental status examination for organic mental symptoms in the elderly patient. In L. Bellak & T. Karasu (Eds.), *Handbook for psychiatrists and family care physicians.* New York: Grune & Stratton.

Ory, M. G. (1994). Dementia special care: The development of a national research initiative. *Alzheimer Disease and Associated Disorders, 8*(Suppl. 1), S389–S404.

Shue, V., Beck, C., & Lawton, M. P. (1996). Measuring affect in frail and cognitively impaired elders. *Journal of Mental Health and Aging, 2,* 259–271.

Tappen, R. M., & Barry, C. (1995). Assessment of affect in advanced Alzheimer's disease: The dementia mood picture test. *Journal of Gerontological Nursing, 21,* 44–46.

6

Enhanced Interdisciplinary Care Planning for Nursing Home Residents with Dementia: Catalyst for Better Care

Kimberly Van Haitsma, Holly Ruckdeschel, Ruth Mooney, Mary Rose Atlas, Jill Etter, Christine Hallahan, Deborah Powell, and Tracy Wills

INTRODUCTION

This chapter describes an enhanced interdisciplinary system of care planning developed at Philadelphia Geriatric Center (PGC). The development of Enhanced Interdisciplinary Care Planning (E-IDCP) was part of a clinical research study on Special Care Units (SCUs) for dementia. An ecological theory of treating dementia served as the basis for the treatment program (Lawton, Van Haitsma, & Klapper, 1994), which was developed on one moderate dementia unit at PGC. The ecological theory of dementia proposes that external sources of environmental stimulation must be appropriately balanced to provide the optimum levels of both challenge and security for the demented individual. The balance between stimulation and security for any demented person can be obtained only when treatment providers take into account that individual's deficits and remaining strengths. Furthermore, because dementia has consequences for the biological, social, and emotional well-being of the person, the focus of treatment must be holistic. For further reporting on this study, see Chapter 5.

This theory of dementia treatment led the SCU study group to focus on the care planning team as the ideal vehicle to provide balanced, holistic assessment and intervention for the individual with dementia. Because of the complexities of dementing process, no one discipline could "own" the issues. It was our goal to develop a treatment team that could comprehensively represent all aspects of the demented individual through open sharing of the talents and insights of a variety of disciplines, cooperative action, and treatment approaches developed in common.

Our initial experience in setting up this new treatment approach led us to conclude that the road to a truly comprehensive and interdisciplinary treatment was not an easy one. The team we began to work with was typical of a nursing home treatment team: membership consisted of a professional nurse, a social worker, an activity therapist, and a dietician; each team member "owned" a piece of the resident's well-being and developed their own treatment approach and goals independently; and care planning meetings were brief with discussions focused primarily on medical issues. As required by Omnibus Reconciliation Act (OBRA) regulations, the Minimum Data Set (MDS) served as the basis for assessment and care planning.

The team needed to learn a new way of thinking about dementia treatment in an ecological context, a different way of working together as disciplines that involved a higher level of interdependence and cohesiveness, and a commitment to increased time for care planning and attention to the functioning of the treatment team itself.

This chapter reflects 3 years' worth of lessons learned both in the benefits of this treatment approach in dementia and the barriers to its application. The SCU study developed the E-IDCP treatment approach on a single dementia unit. At the conclusion of the study, the response from residents, family, and staff was so positive that the administration decided to replicate this approach on all units at PGC in which persons with dementia reside.

In this chapter we outline some key concepts regarding the core components of the E-IDCP approach, the content and process of the care planning session, and some key barriers to application; we also propose solutions to these difficulties.

CORE COMPONENTS OF E-IDCP

Key Concepts of How Teams Work

Interdisciplinary vs. Multidisciplinary Teams. While the conceptual framework of our treatment approach to the demented individual was ecological theory, we found it invaluable to understand theories of how teams of individuals work together effectively (Qualls & Czirr, 1988). Well-functioning treatment teams do not just happen. The development of an interdisciplinary geriatric treatment team can be difficult and requires attention to the intricacies of how groups of individuals learn to work together to provide comprehensive and integrated treatment. Without this knowledge and attention, treatment teams can become inefficient and ineffective. Residents do not receive the quality of care they require and team members find team meetings to be, at best, a waste of time or, at worst, marked by anger, resentment, and anxiety.

Most treatment teams in the nursing home operate using a multidisciplinary or consultative approach. Members of such teams serve as independent consultants who each have a well-defined role within the team. Communication among team members tends to be informal. Each member carries out his or her own assessment and treatment plan and then communicates the results to the other team members. Consultative team models can often result in duplication of services and poorly integrated approaches to the treatment of the demented individual as each team member develops an independent treatment plan.

In contrast, we were seeking to build an interdisciplinary team model. Interdisciplinary teams are characterized by greater interdependence among team members without a hierarchical team organization. Within such teams, members meet together to review all concerns regarding the patient, to develop a method of assessing these concerns, and to generate a treatment plan. Thus, one treatment plan is developed collaboratively that includes input and participation from all members. Once the goals for the resident are agreed upon, team members also work collaboratively toward implementing and achieving these goals.

Necessary Conditions for Interdisciplinary Team Development. Effective interdisciplinary treatment teams are characterized by several key conditions that include an understanding of the mission of the treatment team, knowledge among the team's members of their own role and the roles of other members within the team, a coordinated and cooperative effort to work together to meet the team's goals, and attention to the team's effectiveness in achieving these goals (Czirr & Rappaport, 1984).

- *Charter.* The charter is essentially the reason for the team working together. Items in the charter include the population with whom the team will be working and the overall goals for the team. Knowledge and acceptance of the parameters of the team's charter by all members will greatly reduce potential differences regarding treatment goals. In our case, it was essential that the team understand and define goals that fit within the ecological and quality of life model of treatment for residents with dementia.
- *Interdependence.* Team members must need each other's experience, ability, and commitment to meet the team goals identified in the charter. This became especially important for the new members who were added to the team.
- *Commitment and Accountability.* Team members must be committed to the team approach and the team must be accountable to the larger organizational unit and to its treatment goals. Lack of accountability can be the root of many of the team's difficulties in starting with this new model of care planning. While we discuss this in greater detail in the section entitled "Barriers and Approaches," we should mention that a well-functioning tracking and feedback system is critical to the long-term operation of a treatment team.
- *Motivation and Willingness.* Team members must be willing to critically examine their work and to engage in mutual problem solving.

- *Time.* Team members must be willing to put in the necessary time it takes for a treatment team to develop and to begin functioning efficiently. Most estimates of this time range from 1 to 3 years (Heming, 1988). The actual length of time will depend on such factors as staff turnover, motivation, and basic interpersonal skills of the particular team. It is also important that team members be willing to spend the necessary time to thoroughly discuss each resident's plan of care. Most interdisciplinary teams limit themselves to 20 to 30 minutes per resident.

- *Feedback.* Team members must be willing to both *give* feedback to other team members and to *receive* feedback from other members. This reciprocity in feedback implies that the traditional hierarchical medical model must be set aside to allow for a free flow of information between all levels of staff from the certified nursing assistant (CNA) to the physician.

Team Development. As we mentioned above, the development of a well-functioning team does not happen overnight. As a treatment team begins the process of coming together, certain stages of development have consistently been found to occur. These developments have been conceptualized to fall into four stages: forming, storming, norming, and performing (Qualls & Czirr, 1988).

- *Forming.* The initial stage of any team development follows the decision that a treatment team can serve a common purpose. Once this decision is made, team members concern themselves with rather practical matters (i.e., who will be served, who will be part of the team, etc.). Very little time or attention is spent on thinking about how the team members will work together. Members often feel somewhat apprehensive about the new endeavor and uneasy about working with people from other professions.

- *Storming.* Once the practical issues and the parameters of the team's focus are decided, team members begin working together. It does not take long for process issues to arise. Differences among team members will occur and could include differences in interpersonal style, preferences on how to organize and run a meeting, and different philosophies regarding patient care. The way in which the team handles these differences will be critical to its future. Some teams cannot tolerate differences and dissolve after being unable to manage them. Other teams remain quiet about the differences and factions develop among subgroups within the team. This always affects the team process adversely and ultimately leads to ineffective care. Well-functioning treatment teams develop ways to identify differences, discuss them in a collaborative manner, and find solutions that allow them to work effectively toward their goals. Later in this chapter, we discuss several strategies for dealing with conflict.

• *Norming.* Once the team has developed its ability to manage conflict and disagreement among members, certain norms will develop. These norms will serve as guidelines for conducting team meetings, the roles that various members play in the team, how the team members manage differences, etc. While these norms may be made explicit, more often they remain implicit and are discussed only if broken.

• *Performing.* This stage in the evolution of the team is marked by efficient management of team issues and effective use of the team process in achieving goals. Norms rarely need to be openly discussed and members feel comfortable with their role in the team, working with other team members, and managing differences that arise.

No team can function in the "performing" stage forever. All teams change with time and the changes will affect the process of team members working together. Changes can include new members joining the team, old members leaving, new patient populations being served, changes in care delivery policies on an administrative level, and others. When such changes occur there is often a return to the "norming" stage. That is, change often requires the development of new norms to incorporate the change while maintaining the team's ability to meet its goals. As with any change this process can be difficult. A return to "storming" is not uncommon as members negotiate new ways of working together as a team.

Team Membership

The typical OBRA-regulated team consists of a registered nurse manager (NM), a social worker (SW), an activity therapist (AT), and a dietician. The E-IDCP team expands the typical OBRA-regulated team membership to include a psychologist and a CNA, preferably the

CNA primarily assigned to the resident being care planned. These six disciplines make up the core membership of the team and attend every meeting. Other disciplines can also attend the care planning meeting on an as needed basis: physician or physician assistant, psychiatrist, chaplain, physical therapist, occupational therapist, speech therapist, or even environmental services. The attendance of physicians at care planning meetings can be complicated if the physician is only available on a part-time basis. It can be helpful to have the NM review the persons to be care planned with the physician prior to the meeting so his or her input can be incorporated into the discussion.

It is critical that each core team member understand his or her role and responsibilities in the care planning process. The four roles that are a part of the functioning of each team are as follows: the NM, the team leader, the team member, and the team recorder. The NM is mandated by OBRA to have ultimate responsibility for the care of the resident and for the completion of the Minimum Data Set (MDS). Regarding the E-IDCP meeting, it is the responsibility of the NM to (1) keep an updated listing of the schedule of care planning; (2) notify team members of the schedule; (3) assign CNAs to attend the care planning meeting; (4) make sure information from "off shifts" is available for the E-IDCP meeting; (5) provide feedback after the care planning meeting to all nonattending nursing staff; (6) comply with all regulations pertaining to the timing and completion of the MDS; and (7) take ultimate responsibility for the functioning of the team over time.

Team Leader.   Leadership requires approximately 1 1/2 hours of preparation time prior to the care planning meeting (this may vary depending on how familiar the leader is with the residents and how many residents are scheduled for care planning that day). While leading the team, it is the leaders' responsibility to (1) *Come prepared.* Preparedness manifests itself in many ways, including finding a substitute leader if s/he is unable to attend the E-IDCP meeting, making sure the resident's chart is reviewed prior to the meeting, and bringing the medical charts to the meeting. (2) *Keep track of time.* Time is an important commodity in any setting. It is the leader's responsibility to make sure the meeting starts and ends on time, that the discussions for each resident are contained to the time allotted (except in crisis situations), that adequate time be made for following-up of residents discussed the previous week, and time for the discussion of emergent issues on the unit. Finally, at the end of the meeting the leader should announce who will be care planned the following week. (3) *Follow the enhanced care planning format.* See the section in this chapter entitled "Content of E-IDCP," below, for more details. (4) *Use good leadership skills.* Good leadership skills are essential to the functioning of the meeting. These skills include soliciting input from each discipline; refocusing team members who get off track; encouraging problem solving using the ecological model and a focus on quality of life; using good listening skills in reflecting back what other team members are saying; and, finally, summarizing the plan of action for each resident before moving on the next person to be care planned.

Team Recorder.   The recorder role can be rotated among disciplines or assigned to a given individual on the team. It is the team recorder's responsibility to (1) *Take notes on each resident's action plan.* After the leader summarizes each resident's plan of action, the recorder notes this on the written care plan including a clear specification as to which discipline(s) are taking responsibility for implementation. This form should be given to the NM at the end of the meeting. It is the NM's responsibility to ensure that this form is shared with day-shift CNAs not present at the meeting and off-shift nursing personnel. (2) *Update a "to do" list.* When an intervention from the previous week's care planning session has not been implemented by the following week, the resident and the suggested intervention should be indicated on a "to do" list. Difficulties in implementing the prescribed intervention should be discussed and solutions offered. The listing will remain and be discussed each week until the appropriate implementation of the plan has occurred or the intervention has been modified as approved by the team.

Team Member.   A team member is defined as anyone who is not leading the meeting. It is the team member's responsibility to (1) *Notify the team leader* if he or she is going to be absent that day and relay pertinent information regarding specific residents to another team member or the leader of the team prior to his or her absence and get an update on any new plan of action for a given resident care planned in his or her absence. (2) *Come prepared.* Make sure the appropriate section of the MDS is completed prior to the meeting and entered into the computer. A team member should also be courteous to other team members by being on time for the start of the meeting. (3) *Participate!* Team members are expected to participate in the discussion of the resident being care planned in the following ways: Provide information about the resident specific to his or her discipline's expertise; ask questions about what a certain word or diagnosis means; respectfully disagree if he or she does not believe that another person's perspective is accurate; brainstorm approaches to care within *or* outside of his/her discipline's traditional scope (e.g., SW (social worker) suggests a nursing intervention, nursing suggests an activity intervention, etc.). (4) *Follow through on assigned tasks.* When accepting responsibility for the implementation of a specific plan of action for a resident, a team member should follow through on the plan within 1 week's time and report the results to the team at the next week's care planning meeting. If the team member is experiencing difficulties, he or she should ask the team for assistance in rethinking the plan of action for that resident. (5) *Support the team.* Team members should realize that team work sometimes means that all members won't completely agree with a given plan of action. Members should try to maintain a positive, try-it-and-see attitude, then give the approach an *honest* attempt. If it does not work, nothing has been lost; in fact, the attempt can encourage a discussion to rethink the situation based on what has been learned.

Leadership Rotation

Leadership of the interdisciplinary team meeting rotates on a 5-week schedule among core disciplines. The change in leadership provides new perspectives to the care planning process, promotes involvement and participation by all disciplines, helps to equalize responsibility for administrative aspects of care planning, increases understanding of residents from a holistic perspective, and increases communication between disciplines both in and out of care planning.

Feedback Mechanisms

Information needs to flow in two directions in order to successfully interweave team care planning and care delivery. First, information—

including current status, problems, and concerns about residents—must flow from the care delivery staff to the E-IDCP team to design useful care plans. Second, new care plan information must flow back from the E-IDCP team to the care delivery staff including all other CNAs not present at E-IDCP meeting, and all staff from the other shifts (CNAs and licensed practical nurses (LPNs) on 3 to 11 p.m. and 11 p.m. to 7 a.m. and weekend shifts.)

Information to the Team.   It is useful to have a checklist for information about a resident's physical, functional, social, and emotional well-being across all shifts on the same piece of paper. This establishes a flow of information from the off-shift nursing personnel to the care planning team. It also (1) assures contributions from all shifts, (2) standardizes the information requested, and (3) eliminates redundancy. The cross-shift checklist should be completed by a care manager from each shift in the week prior to the E-IDCP meeting. The NM is responsible for sharing pertinent off-shift nursing staff problems, approaches, or other helpful information during the E-IDCP meeting.

During the E-IDCP meeting, a useful tool for keeping track of residents is to utilize a chalkboard or large poster paper divided into four sections entitled: "Residents for care planning in current week"; "Residents care planned in previous week"; "Residents to be care planned the next week"; "Residents for ad hoc discussion" (team members, when coming in for the meeting, can add names to this list). A visible list helps the team leader and members budget amounts of time for each resident and facilitates the follow-up of residents care planned the week before. If a resident continues to require follow-up because the situation has still not been resolved to all team members' satisfaction, the team recorder will note that individual's name and provide follow-up until the situation is resolved.

Information from the E-IDCP Team.   Following the meeting information needs to be communicated *back to* the care delivery staff. To accomplish this, the NM selects key points from her handwritten notes of each resident's care planning session and highlights them with a marker. These notes, along with those from other residents whose care was planned that day, are attached to nursing staff meeting forms. The NM reviews the highlighted areas with day shift CNAs in a meeting to be held within 2 days of E-IDCP meeting. CNAs are responsible for reading the highlighted material and signing off on the care planning form.

Feedback to other shifts occurs by off-shift LPNs reviewing the care planning notes in a weekly post-care planning meeting with her or his CNA staff. The LPN assures that CNAs read and sign off on meeting notes as well. The LPN returns the meeting forms to the RN for distribution to the other shifts.

Attention to Process

In order for any team to function effectively, time must be set aside for focusing on how the team works together as a group. Because it is difficult to focus on the process of care planning while actually doing it, we recommend setting aside a special meeting time to focus specifically on process. "Process meetings" can be called at any time, by any team member, but they should definitely be held within 6 to 8 weeks after a team has initiated E-IDCP and at least every 6 months after that. In cases where a team may be stuck in the "storming" stage, it is helpful to have a designated facilitator in the facility to help the team in getting unstuck. The facilitator can serve several functions: (1) to mentor and educate new team members; (2) to help in quality assurance procedures regarding care planning; and (3) to assist in conflict resolution. It is the facilitator's responsibility to attend to the process of the group (e.g., how well the members are working as a team), not the specific content of the care planning. The facilitator schedules the process meeting and leads the team in a brainstorming session to find resolution to the difficulties. It is paramount that the facilitator ensure that a safe, constructive, supportive discussion is maintained during the meeting, provide consistent feedback to all team members about what they are doing well, and summarize the approaches identified to rectify the difficulties. Team building exercises can be helpful in facilitating conflict resolution. Good resources for this can be found in Mariano (1989) and Heming (1988).

CONTENT OF CARE PLANNING SESSION

The care planning session of a nursing home resident uses the Minimum Data Set (MDS). The care planning session for a given resident is initiated by identifying the purpose of the review (annual, quarterly, readmission following a hospitalization). This is followed by a short description of the resident's psychosocial history, medical diagnoses, medications, and a review of the MDS triggers. The leader solicits input regarding problematic issues for the resident and encourages a brainstorming approach to interventions with the resident within the framework of the ecological model of treatment for dementia. Approaches are then summarized and incorporated into the plan of care by the recorder.

CASE STUDY

The following case study is presented to illustrate the functioning of the team to solve problems related to the care of a resident. It was based on problems that have actually occurred. The resident's characteristics do not refer to an individual resident but are drawn from a compilation of residents. Mrs. L., a 94-year-old woman, resided on a unit for the mildly cognitively impaired.

Social History.   Mrs. L. was born in Russia and was one of six siblings. Her family immigrated to the United States when she was an infant. She has an elementary school education. She married at age 19, raised two children, and was a homemaker. When her husband died in 1970, she resided independently for quite some time. She enjoyed card games, casino trips, and walking. She moved into an assisted living residence in 1982. She later moved to the nursing home because her cognitive status had declined.

Medical History.   Atonic bladder (history of indwelling catheter for at least 2 years), dementia of unknown etiology, congestive heart failure (CHF), hypertension (HTN), ischemic cardiomyopathy, depression, chronic constipation, and a history of breast cancer. Her medications included benazepril HCR (Lotensin: antihypertensive); bumetanide (Bumex: diuretic and treatment of CHF); Lanoxin (digoxin: treatment of CHF); buspirone (Buspar: antianxiety); Colace (stool softener); and lactulose (laxative). This was a quarterly care planning session for Mrs. L.

Following admission to the nursing home, Mrs. L. resided on a unit whose residents (for the most part) were generally socially appropriate. She was displaying behavior considered problematic by staff and other residents. These behaviors included noncompliance with continence care, poor personal hygiene, and spitting.

These behaviors were not socially acceptable on this unit. Families and other residents were complaining to the social worker about Mrs. L.'s odor, due to poor hygiene, and her spitting. Although Mrs. L. had a Foley catheter, she also wore a protective garment because of her fecal incontinence. If this became soiled, she would often remove it and leave it in a public rest room. She might then have "accidents" with no protective garment on. Staff in public areas of the facility were complaining several times a week that Mrs. L.'s accidents were putting all the residents, staff, and visitors "at risk for slipping in both urine and stool."

There were strong "suggestions" from these individuals that Mrs. L. should be moved to a gated unit where she would not be allowed to wander to a public space. (In this facility, gated units are used to protect residents who wander or are an elopement risk from becoming lost.) However, the activity Mrs. L. enjoyed most was walking. She ambulated freely around the nursing home, including public areas. She stayed within a limited boundary and did not intrude in areas where she did not belong, such as clinics and other units. If she were on a gated unit, she would be unable to travel freely. The argument for having her on a gated unit was that her "accidents" would be limited to the care floor, where they could be readily detected by staff and dealt with. Also, it was argued that residents on gated units are generally more confused and might not be as disturbed by Mrs. L.'s behavior.

The social worker (SW) voiced a growing sense of frustration among nurses about this problem. They were ready to have the problem resident moved off the floor—they were tired of having "the whole nursing home" calling them to complain.

The social worker and psychologist were concerned that moving Mrs. L. to a gated unit would cause her to be separated from the one friend she had on the unit where she resided. It would also cause her to feel more confused because of the change in environment. The team expressed the belief that she would soon learn to open the gate, thus making her relocation ineffective.

Her daughter was embarrassed and upset by her poor hygiene and soiling. She was also extremely fearful and would not consent to a room change to a gated unit.

Interventions That Were in Place. The SW undertook the following interventions before the E-IDCP meeting: (1) One-to-one with Mrs. L. once a week to remind her of the importance of wearing her incontinence garment and to use tissues if she needed to spit; (2) redirection of Mrs. L. back to unit when she was observed without a protective garment; (3) work with the care planning team to constantly provide Mrs. L. with tissues and a bag in which to dispose of them; (4) work with Mrs. L's daughter to help find a protective garment in which Mrs. L. would feel more comfortable. The SW also asked Mrs. L.'s daughter to reinforce the management plan during interactions with her mother; and (5) the SW spoke with various staff around the nursing home at least once per week to reassure them that the care team was trying to address this problem and requested their help in implementing the plan for redirecting Mrs. L. back to unit as necessary.

The nursing staff performed the following interventions prior to the E-IDCP meeting: (1) developed a toileting schedule that was employed to reduce incontinence incidents and (2) gave Mrs. L. more frequent baths to improve hygiene.

Other concerns included Mrs. L.'s mild depression, for which she was seen by a psychologist for therapy every 2 to 3 weeks. Previously, she had been seen once or twice a week for psychotherapy when her depressive symptoms were more pronounced. Her wandering and short attention span also contributed to her failure to eat enough and to her significant weight loss. She frequently left the dining room without finishing her meal. Although she was restless and wandered, she did attend certain activities on the unit, such as weekly religious services (for the entire 30 minutes), monthly birthday parties (for about 15 minutes), and bingo twice a week. However, due to her incontinence, odor, and disheveled appearance, some residents often stated, "Don't let her sit near me." When she spit on the floor, other residents complained and the group was interrupted to remind Mrs. L. to use her tissues and/or her bag. When Mrs. L. saw the activity therapist taking other residents out on group trips she would ask, "how come I'm not going?" It was considered inappropriate to take her on trips out of the facility.

Despite all of the interventions already in place, Mrs. L. continued to spend time off the unit in common areas with soiled clothing, and there were incontinence incidents that posed perceived health and safety risks to other residents and staff. Mrs. L. did not remember to keep her protective garment on despite frequent reminders from staff. Pressure from the administration was mounting to improve the situation or Mrs. L. would be moved to a unit that would restrict her from walking freely within the facility.

Interventions Agreed on at the E-IDCP Meeting.   After reviewing her psychosocial history, diagnoses, medications, and the MDS, the team brainstormed regarding Mrs. L.'s problematic behaviors. The team strongly suspected that Mrs. L.'s dementia was progressing and that her poor hygiene and weight loss reflected the fact that Mrs. L. was overchallenged and needed a more supportive environment to allow her to maintain a higher level of functioning. In addition, the team felt it important to rule out the possibility of a medical cause for her behavior. Therefore, several interventions were put into place: (1) Mrs. L. was referred to a gerontological clinical nurse specialist (CNS) who noted her urological history and performed a thorough assessment. Mrs. L. was having periodic leaking around the catheter that the CNS thought this might be due to bladder contractions, not bladder atony. A referral was written for Mrs. L. to see the urologist. The CNS and Mrs. L.'s daughter accompanied her to the appointment. It was decided to remove the catheter and check for residual several times to make sure she did not experience retention. (2) The team also decided to implement the use of a pant-and-pad system that she could manage more easily. Her toileting schedule was re-evaluated and the frequency of prompting Mrs. L. to use the bathroom was increased by all staff. (3) Mrs. L. was redirected back in the dining room at mealtime and encouraged to finish her meals. She was also offered sandwiches she could eat "on the go" between meals; and (4) the frequency of reminding Mrs. L. to use a supplied tissue and bag to spit into was increased by all staff.

At a Follow-Up Care Planning Meeting.   At her next quarterly review, Mrs. L.'s frequency of incontinence was greatly reduced. She asked staff for assistance with changing less frequently. She no longer removed her garment in the public rest room. She had no problems with retention of urine. Although she occasionally had an "accident" in a public area, the frequency was much less. The pressure to move Mrs. L. to a gated unit had abated.

Redirection back to the dining room and "on the go" snacks resulted in a stabilization of Mrs. L.'s weight. Mrs. L. used tissues and bag regularly for spitting after being prompted to do so. She has continued to be able to ambulate freely throughout the nursing home and seems content. Her daughter was happy with the outcome and relieved that her mother still has her freedom. The team takes pride in their "success" and gets a sense of accomplishment when they see her in public areas of the facility.

BENEFITS OF E-IDCP

Several benefits of enhanced interdisciplinary care planning have been identified. Members of the care planning team have been observed to interact throughout the care planning process rather than "turn taking" as practiced in ordinary multidisciplinary care planning. Team members helped each other find information in the medical chart when needed. They also all contributed to problem solving regarding areas of concern rather than viewing problems as the responsibility of one discipline. For example, weight loss was previously viewed as a nursing concern because nursing assistants feed and weigh residents. In E-IDCP, the activity therapist may make observations about how and what a resident eats in activities as well as in regular meals. The social worker may comment on other residents the individual likes best and suggest seating arrangements to make mealtime a more social occasion. The dietitian will review food preferences, suggest adaptive equipment, finger foods, or other food modifications. Through the interaction, more people become aware of the range of possibilities and are soon seen making these suggestions across disciplines.

Over time the E-IDCP process facilitates a comprehensive foundation of knowledge of the whole person rather than isolated aspects of the individual. The goal of E-IDCP is holistic rather than fragmented care. Some disciplines were not aware of the signs and symptoms of various diseases, how diseases impact on the persons ability to function, and the purpose of specific medications or the side effects of medications. Other disciplines were not aware of the resident's social background, including previous work history, family, and leisure activities. Although these have always been presented in care planning, team members now listen more carefully and ask questions when they do not understand the information that is being presented. CNAs shed light on what the individual can do, their likes and dislikes, and hints and tips to get the individual to complete needed tasks. Activity therapists often see a very different side of the individual and are able to share likes and dislikes with the team. In one care planning session, the activity therapist suggested that a resident might have a recurrence of a urinary tract infection based on the observation that there had been a change in his behavior. Previously, nursing or medicine were the only disciplines who would make that kind of observation.

E-IDCP members have become more committed and involved in care planning, have developed better skills in the leadership role, and experience better working relationships both within and outside the care planning meeting. Members come to care planning better prepared. They know that they have valuable information about the resident and that the other team members will listen to and consider what they have to say. There is a development of increased understanding and respect for other disciplines' knowledge and responsibilities. Team members use each other in a consultative manner. There is a real attempt to understand what the other person is saying and add that information to their own knowledge base rather than view areas as "belonging" to another discipline and therefore something they do not need to be concerned about.

Part of the enhanced care planning approach includes follow-up each week on progress toward decisions made during care planning the previous week. This responsibility falls to the individual who led the care planning session. Previously, this responsibility was either not assigned or fell to nursing. This sharing of responsibility for follow-up of decisions made regarding care has spread the burden of carrying out the decisions. Fixing responsibility and providing a mechanism for reporting back has resulted in more decisions being implemented. If difficulties are encountered in implementing the decision, the team can engage in further problem solving and perhaps offer different suggestions to address the issue. Under the previous system, follow-up may not occur until the next quarterly care planning session. Collaborative decision making leads to an increased involvement in treatment decisions not specific to one discipline evolved. All team members develop an increased sense of responsibility for carrying out all aspects of the care plan. For example, when a behavioral intervention is suggested, all team members assist with the development of the plan; therefore they all have an interest in seeing the plan be successful. With all team members implementing the behavioral plan, it has a greater chance of success. Also if team members find the intervention is not working, they are more likely to bring it back to care planning for further evaluation and revision.

BARRIERS AND APPROACHES

As we mentioned at the beginning of the chapter, enacting a shift from a multidisciplinary approach to an enhanced interdisciplinary approach is no easy task. The most common difficulties are goal conflicts, value conflicts, process of decision-making conflicts, interpersonal conflicts, institutional barriers, lack of follow-up, and poor leadership skills (Drinka & Streim, 1994; Mariano, 1989). We have found it helpful to review this list in process meetings to aid in focusing discussions on difficulties in the functioning of the team. Each barrier is discussed in turn and suggested approaches in dealing with each are reviewed.

Goal Conflict.   Team members may have conflicting goals about the functioning of the team. One team member may be focusing on the short-term goals, while another is focusing on the long term. It is helpful to have each team member clearly state their goals and then have discussions as to the priorities of the goals expressed.

Value Conflict.   Team members may have dissimilar philosophies that may lead to conflict. For example, one team member may embrace a "maintenance or comfort care" approach to care for a demented nursing home resident, whereas another team member may espouse a "restorative" approach. It is helpful for the team to identify the different values represented in the room and have an open and noncritical discussion of how these philosophies get translated into care decisions.

Process of Resolving Decision-Making Conflicts. The team may be having difficulties in making truly interdisciplinary decisions for a variety of reasons. The team may be unclear about what the problem really is, making decisions without sufficient data, accepting the first option voiced rather than weighing several options, discounting the assessments of certain team members, or failing to agree upon who should be responsible for the approaches discussed.

Finally, they might have differing points of view as to the "logic of assessment" (Qualls & Czirr, 1988). One team member may think of assessment as a "rule out" where hypotheses are systematically eliminated until a single problem and matching solution are found. Another team member may be thinking of assessment as a "rule in" where the field of view is enlarged to encompass an increasingly broad range of factors and environmental interactions.

Helpful approaches to these barriers include defining problems in specific, behavioral terms by describing what is happening, when, and in what context; clarifying the necessity of each team member's involvement in the decision-making process, with an emphasis on respect for all members' contributions and expertise; leading the team through the process of weighing all of the options in light of the needs of the resident, the needs of the unit as a whole, and demands of institution; obtaining commitment to specific action with specified responsibilities for who will follow through on these actions; and encouraging a "rule in" approach that takes into account the complex web of physical, social, environmental, and emotional factors that are at play. Last, a positive, try-it-and-see attitude must be cultivated. Approaches can be ordered and implemented sequentially—if the first one doesn't work, try the second.

Interpersonal Conflict. Interpersonal conflicts are very commonplace in the dynamics of even highly functional teams. Turnover in personnel, job and personal stresses, and a constantly changing regulatory environment can all help to create fertile ground for interpersonal difficulties between team members. Team members may engage in power struggles, be dominated by certain individuals, be driven by hidden agendas, or undermined by sabotage (Drinka & Streim, 1994).

If these interpersonal conflicts begin to interfere with care delivery to the patient, they must be sorted out either on an individual basis or in a team process meeting.

It is helpful to encourage a respectful confrontation of the mal-adaptive conflicts. The discussion should be frank and constructive, focusing on concrete examples of the issues and not broad personal assaults on character. Attention should be drawn to the differences between a team member's words and his or her actions or between a team member's behavior and the institution's policy. Be aware that severe interpersonal conflicts may require mediation by a neutral facilitator from outside the team context.

Institutional Barriers.   Conflicts on teams may be traced to difficulties on an institutional level. For example, if the team is being pressured to shorten the care planning session, the result could be premature shutdown of the decision-making process. Upper management must support the structural changes that enhanced interdisciplinary care planning brings with it: usually an increase in the amount of care planning time (about 20 to 30 minutes per resident) and the atten-dance of enhanced team membership (CNAs, psychologist, physician assistant). Help for institutional barriers should be persistently sought from each team member's supervisor.

Lack of Follow-up on Approaches.   Another difficulty frequently encoun-tered is a lack of follow-through after the treatment approaches had been decided upon. Well-thought-out and agreed-upon approaches can often go untried or lost in the bustle of day to day life on the unit.

We found three techniques helpful in optimizing follow-through: (1) Obtaining commitment to specific action with specified responsi-bilities for who will follow through on these actions in the care planning session, (2) During the care planning session, taking time to review new treatment approaches for the individuals discussed the previous week. If approaches have not been attempted, or have been attempted and failed, taking time to reopen the discussion about the plan of care. (3) Weekly review of a running "to do" list of suggested interventions and approaches which get read at every care planning session. Approaches get crossed off the list when they appear to be functioning well and have been thoroughly incorporated into the plan of care.

Poor Leadership/Team Member Skills.   One cannot stress enough the importance of appropriate training in E-IDCP in facilitating the skills of the team members. A team mentor from any discipline must be designated to train new teams and to train new team members as turnover occurs. The mentor observes each team on a biannual basis to review each teams progress toward achieving and maintaining the standards of care planning. The mentor should track teams as they go through the training process and provide teams with verbal and written feedback regarding their performance. This individual should also attend a new team's first process meeting and provide a written summary of the team's status to each team member and to administration. If the mentor notes that a particular team member is struggling, they should approach that member individually to provide feedback and suggestions for improvement.

SUMMARY

In summary, this chapter has sought to provide an overview of the development of E-IDCP for persons with dementia who reside in nursing homes. In our experience with E-IDCP, we have found the quality of care delivery to persons with dementia to be greatly enhanced by providing teams with education regarding a holistic and ecological theory of dementia, training in specific aspects of the process of interdisciplinary group functioning, enhancing team membership with other disciplines, rotating team leadership, and specifying the necessary aspects of the content of the care planning session. A case study was presented to illustrate the enhanced interdisciplinary processes in action. In addition, we reviewed the benefits of this approach and some of the barriers to effective team functioning. It is our hope that the reading of this chapter will enable care providers to take elements of our experience to strengthen the quality of care provided to persons with dementia in their facilities.

ACKNOWLEDGMENTS

Special thanks to members of the first Enhanced Interdisciplinary Care Planning Team whose hard work and dedication made this concept come to life: Alicia Abel, David Sprenkel, and Susan Flacker. This project was supported by generous contributions from the National Institute on Aging Special Care Cooperative Study (U01-10304), the Alzheimer's Association, and the Harry Stern Family and Joseph Abramson Family Alzheimer's Research Program.

REFERENCES

Czirr, R., & Rappaport, M. (1984). Toolkit for teams: Annotated bibliography on interdisciplinary health teams. *Clinical Gerontologist, 2,* 47–54.

Drinka, T. J., & Streim, J. E. (1994). Case studies from purgatory: Maladaptive behavior within geriatric health care teams. *The Gerontologist, 34,* 541–547.

Heming, D. (1988). The titanic triumvirate: Teams, teamwork, teambuilding. *Canadian Journal of Occupational Therapy,* Feb., 15–20.

Lawton, M. P., Van Haitsma, K. S., & Klapper, J. A. (1994). A balanced stimulation-retreat program for a special care dementia unit. *Alzheimer's Disease and Related Disorders: An International Journal, 8,* S133–138.

Mariano, C. (1989). The case for interdisciplinary collaboration. *Nursing Outlook,* Nov./Dec., 285–288.

Qualls, S. H., & Czirr, R. (1988). Geriatric health teams: Classifying models of professional and team functioning. *The Gerontologist, 28,* 372–376.

7

Family Caregiving: Change, Continuity, and Diversity

Rhonda J. V. Montgomery and Karl D. Kosloski

Surprisingly, there is evidence that gerontologists called for training of caregivers for the elderly as early as the sixteenth century. Yet, the centrality of family members as the key providers of long-term care for impaired elders and the need of these family members for assistance and support in the caregiving role has emerged as a social problem only over the past two decades. Prior to that time, the care of impaired persons remained a "personal trouble" (Mills, 1959), which was resolved through the means of economic incentives for family members, personal responsibility, or, as a last resort, welfare mechanisms such as the almshouse. Family caregiving has emerged as a public issue because of the increased number of persons who are living to be older and who experience extended periods of chronic disability. Hence, the dependency needs of older persons today have shifted from the primarily economic to the physical, and the presence of these needs has become more prevalent and consequently more normative. In the absence of a societal solution to this growing public, the physical dependence of the elderly has

An earlier version of this paper was presented at the Alzheimer's Disease Caregiving Institute's Annual Conference, Case Western Reserve University, Cleveland, OH: April, 1995.

remained a private trouble to be confronted largely by family members who serve as caregivers.

For large numbers of caregivers, this private trouble is particularly challenging because they must deal with issues of memory loss in addition to limitations of physical functioning. Although there are no precise estimates of the total number of people suffering from Alzheimer's disease, what is known with certainty is that the number is expected to grow precipitously in coming years. An overwhelming risk factor of the disease is age, and those over the age of 85 represent the fastest-growing segment of the adult population (Henig, 1996). Currently Alzheimer's disease is estimated to affect about 5% of the population 65 and older, and the prevalence estimates for persons 85 and older range from 20 to 47% (Cox, 1996; Evans et al., 1990).

This emergence of caregiving as a social problem has been both heralded and prompted by the proliferation of a huge literature that has documented the central role of family members in the provision of long-term care and the health, social, and psychological consequences of caregiving for these family members. Early work on caregivers tended to treat caregiving as a singular role; but in time, inconsistent findings from small local samples and the descriptive findings from national samples revealed the diversity of the caregiving role. Despite some descriptive consistencies the literature, such as the prevalence of wives and daughters as caregivers, there are also numerous inconsistencies in the literature regarding the characteristics of caregivers (Stone, 1991); the type of care normally provided (Matthews & Rosner, 1988); the consequences of caregiving for caregivers and elders; and the impact of interventions designed to assist caregivers (Zarit, 1990). In fact, the inconsistencies within the literature are so basic that even the term *caregiver* has no common meaning (Stone, 1991).

The purpose of this paper is to present a conceptual framework that can provide a clarifying lens to identify consistencies within the mosaic of diversity of caregiving experiences and activities and guide the design and targeting of appropriate interventions. The model is viewed as particularly useful for understanding variations in the caregiving trajectory of family members providing care for persons with Alzheimer's disease.

DIVERSITY OF CAREGIVING

Who Are the Caregivers?

Although there tends to be a general consensus that the majority of caregivers are women, there has actually been great variation among study findings in the reported distribution of caregivers between the two sexes and among family members. The variation tends to stem from differences in the definition of caregiving tasks (Stone, 1991) and the sampling process (Montgomery & Kosloski, 1994). When caregiving is defined to include the full range of helping tasks—from visiting and occasional assistance with chores to intense personal care—study samples tend to include a broader range of family and friends with greater representation of males and more distant relatives. In contrast, studies that use more limited definitions that focus on activities of daily living (ADLs) tend to report a larger proportion of women and of spouses.

The general consensus in the literature is that, most often, one family member serves as the primary source of care for an impaired elderly person, although others in the network of family and friends may serve as "secondary caregivers." The greater concentration of women and daughters as caregivers in samples that include the more impaired elders likely reflects the fact that these helpers are primary rather than secondary caregivers (Merrill, 1997; Stern, 1996). It has also become widely recognized that there are consistent patterns in the selection of the primary caregiver that are associated with family relationships, gender, and living arrangements of the family members (Cantor, 1979; Cicirelli, 1992; Horowitz, 1985; Lee, 1992; Matthews, 1995; Merrill, 1997). When available, a spouse provides the majority of care. In the absence of a spouse, a daughter is most likely to assume the role. In the absence of a daughter, a son will assume the role, although there is considerable evidence that sons transfer many care tasks to their spouses. In the absence of offspring, other, more distant family members become responsible. The caregiver role also tends to fall to the person with the fewest competing responsibilities, including obligations to the spouse, children, and employees (Brody, 1990; Stern, 1996; Stueve & O'Donnell, 1989). The

implications of this ordered pattern of selection for prevalence estimates of caregivers can be illustrated using the data from the 1982
Caregiver supplement to the National Long Term Care Survey
(Stone, Cafferata, & Sangl, 1997). When the data include both primary and secondary caregivers, women make up 72% of the sample
and spouses represent 36%. Of the total, 29% of the caregivers are
daughters; 8% are sons; 20% are other females, and 7% are other
male relatives. When the data are restricted to primary caregivers
only, women continue to make up almost three-quarters (74%) of
caregivers, but representation of spouses increases to almost half
(48%) of the caregivers in the sample. This increase in spouses is
offset by a decrease in the proportion of sons, who represent only
6% of the sample primary caregivers, and a decrease in other females
(14%) and other males (3%). Daughters are equally represented
among primary (29%) and secondary caregivers (30%).

The second factor that leads to inconsistent findings regarding the
prevalence of different family members as caregivers is the sampling
frame. The sampling process for the majority of studies of caregivers
is to first identify a sample of impaired elders and then identify the
caregivers of these elders. This mechanism creates a bias toward
caregivers who are caring for significantly impaired elders. Consequently, studies using this mechanism tend to be biased toward
primary caregivers who have been providing care for an extended
period of time. In contrast, a few studies have sampled adult children
and asked about the types of care that they provide for parents.
This process results in samples of caregivers that include persons
providing minimal assistance for less impaired elders. Studies using
this sampling process adopt implicitly a definition of caregiving that
is not distinct from familial assistance that may take place in the
absence of a disability. Notably these samples tend to include more
males and reveal fewer gender differences in the types of helping
tasks performed (Stoller, Forster, & Duniho, 1992).

Patterns in Task Performance

Although a child might serve as a substitute source of care, there is
considerable evidence that there are dramatic differences between
the types of tasks that children perform as caregivers and those that

spouses perform. There are also differences between spouses and children in the intensity of tasks and the length of time that care tasks are performed. Spouses who identify themselves as caregivers report between 40 and 60 hours performing caregiving tasks depending upon the sample (Montgomery & Datwyler, 1990; Merrill, 1997; Spitze & Logan, 1990). Moreover, the majority of these hours are devoted to household chores, meal preparation and personal care such as bathing, dressing and toileting. In contrast, studies that have included significant numbers of adult children report that the average amount of time that children spend performing care tasks is one-third to one-half as much time as reported for spouses. In addition, children tend to concentrate more of their time doing care management tasks and assisting with transportation and shopping (Montgomery & Datwyler, 1990). This is especially true for sons. Children not only provide less care and less intensive care, they tend to provide assistance for shorter periods of time (Stone et al., 1987; Montgomery & Kosloski, 1994; Johnson & Catalano, 1983; Montgomery & Kamo, 1989; Montgomery, Kosloski, & Datwyler, 1993). In part, these differences between spouses and children in type and intensity of the care they provide reflects differences in living arrangement. In the case of spouses, virtually all care recipients reside with the caregiver and consequently perform a wide range of care tasks as part of their everyday activities. This is not necessarily the case for adult children for whom separate residence is more common. However, the living arrangement does not fully account for all of the observed differences reported in many studies focused on the most dependent population, because a large proportion of adult children in these studies do reside in the same household as the care recipient (e.g., Montgomery et al., 1993).

Care Sharing

Spouses and adult children who are primary caregivers also differ in the way they share care responsibilities with other family members who may participate in the caregiving process as backup or secondary sources of care (Coward & Dwyer, 1990; Montgomery et al., 1993; Montgomery & Kamo, 1989; Tennstedt, McKinlay, & Sullivan, 1989). When the primary caregiver is a spouse, secondary caregivers are most likely to be adult children. When the primary caregiver is a child, secondary caregivers tend to be the spouses or siblings of the primary caregiver (Montgomery et al., 1993).

Regardless of who the second caregiver is, spouses tend to perform 80% or more of the care tasks (Stoller, 1992; Johnson & Catalano, 1983; Montgomery & Kamo, 1989). The care provided by secondary caregivers tends to account for a smaller proportion of the overall care and tends to complement the care tasks of the spouse, which are usually concentrated on personal care and household chores. As secondary caregivers, children concentrate their efforts on tasks that are more consistent with their role as children, such as help with transportation, banking, and paperwork or sporadic household and yard maintenance activities. There is, however, some variation with the sex of the child who is a second caregiver. Daughters tend to provide more care of every type except help with legal and banking tasks than do sons; daughters also tend to provide more routine care and distribute their hours more evenly across the various types of tasks (Johnson & Catalano, 1983; Montgomery et al., 1993; Montgomery & Kamo, 1989; Tennstedt et al., 1989; Coward & Dwyer, 1990). Sons tend to concentrate their efforts on tasks that are more circumscribed and sporadic, such as occasional shopping trips or annual yard and house maintenance activities (Matthews & Rosner, 1988; Montgomery et al., 1993). This pattern is most pronounced for sons who are secondary caregivers for their mothers. Sons as secondary care-givers provide less assistance to mothers than to fathers and they provide almost no help for mothers with personal care. Montgomery and her colleagues (1993) report that the assistance provided by sons accounted for only 3.2% of the care that their mother received, in contrast to the 22.4% of care that daughters provided as second caregivers.

Despite their greater work load, spouses are also the least likely among caregivers to seek and use formal support services (Stoller, 1992). This tendency is most pronounced for wives, who tend to resist outside support to a greater degree than do husbands (Stoller, 1992; Stone et al., 1987; Tennstedt et al., 1989).

In contrast to the care-sharing patterns observed for spouses who are primary caregivers, adult children who are primary caregivers tend to share care tasks more equally with secondary caregivers. When both the primary and secondary caregiving roles are assumed by children, secondary caregivers tend to do similar tasks as primary caregivers and distribute their caregiving time among the various tasks in a similar manner. Consequently, the assistance provided by secondary caregivers in this family constellation tends to supplement the care provided by the primary caregivers (Montgomery et al., 1993; Stoller, 1992; Tennstedt et al., 1989). Again, however, the sex of the caregivers involved tends to be associated with the patterns of care sharing. As primary caregivers, daughters provided a greater percentage of total care than did son primary caregivers. Primary and secondary caregivers tend to share the care load almost equally when the primary caregiver is a son (Merrill, 1996). Sons also tend to receive more assistance form formal service providers than do daughters (Merrill, 1997; Wright, 1983). Moreover, secondary caregivers tend to provide the greatest proportion of the elder's total care and the greatest amount of personal care when they are assisting primary caregivers who are the opposite sex of the elder (Lawton, Silverstein, & Bengtson, 1994; Montgomery et al., 1993).

DISCERNING CONSISTENCY IN DIVERSITY

A Conceptual Framework

The conceptual framework of caregiving careers presented here has been formulated as a mechanism within which to interpret the diverse and sometimes conflicting findings regarding prevalence of caregivers, the types and intensity of tasks they perform, and the consequences of this care for the caregivers (Kosloski & Montgomery, 1993). The framework is particularly useful for understanding variations in the care patterns and support needs of persons caring for family members who have Alzheimer's disease or other dementias because it emphasizes the importance of familial roles and family histories for understanding the care context. Grounded in role theory, this framework recognizes caregiving as a unique dynamic process that nevertheless has uniform markers denoting shifts from one stage to another. The framework is useful because (1) the identification of salient features of the caregiving process is an essential component of the broader goal of understanding dyadic relationships in general and (2) charting the caregiving career has implications for development and implementation of interventions and practices to effectively support families in their caregiving efforts.

The framework rests on two key premises. First, there is no single, generic caregiver role, but rather caregiving is a role that emerges from prior role relationships. It is influenced by the unique values, beliefs, and circumstances of the role occupant. Consequently, as with other social roles, there are both consistencies in the process and unique adaptations. Second, caregiving is a dynamic process that unfolds over time and has been likened to a career of variable length (Montgomery & Hatch, 1987; Pearlin, 1992; Knight, Lutzky, & Macofsky-Urban, 1993). As such, each caregiving history has (1) a beginning, (2) some definable temporal extension or duration, and (3) an end or resolution (e.g., recovery, death, or nursing home placement).

Emergent Role.   Because the caregiving role is an emergent role that evolves out of another pre-existing familial role, individuals assume the caregiver role and perform in that role in a manner that is consistent with the expectations and obligations that accompany the initial role the caregiver has in relationship to the elder (e.g., the role of spouse, son, daughter or other relative). Consequently, both the obligations and the expectations that a caregiver has as a spouse, a daughter, or a son, influence how and to what extent he or she assists the impaired relative and the consequences that a caregiver experiences as a result of his or her caregiving behaviors.

Clearly within our society, the marital relationship is fundamentally different from the parent-child relationship in its history, expectations, level of commitment, patterns of costs and rewards, and duration. Spousal caregiving emerges out of a reciprocal relationship where two persons have historically shared responsibility for each other's welfare and have voluntarily made a personal and legal commitment to care for one another. In contrast, the parent-child relationship has historically been asymmetrical in terms of responsibility. The parent has a moral and legal obligation to care for the child. Although, as the child becomes an adult, this relationship shifts from one of dependency for the child, parent-child relationships throughout the life cycle tend to remain asymmetrical, with care and assistance passing from parent to child until the parent becomes impaired (Pearlin, 1992). In combination with gender and cultural norms regarding the division of household labor and kin care, these differences in the initial dyadic relationship are reflected in consistent patterns that have been observed in (1) prevalence of different types of caregivers (Cantor, 1979; Cicirelli, 1992; Stone et al., 1987), (2) the types of tasks performed (Finley, 1989; Lee, 1992; Merrill, 1997; Stone et al., 1987; Walker & Pratt, 1991; Montgomery, 1992), (3) the length of time that care is provided (Montgomery & Kosloski, 1994; Stoller, 1992), and (4) variations in the experience of caregiver stress and burden (Kleban, Brody, Schoonover, & Hoffman, 1989; Montgomery & Datwyler, 1990; Stoller, 1992; Stoller & Pugliesi, 1989).

Caregiving as a Dynamic Process.   Even though caregiving can be described in temporal units, the passage of time per se is unlikely to be an adequate descriptor of the caregiving situation. Tremendous variation exists in the trajectory of caregiving careers, which a simple measure of time cannot reflect. This variation in caregiving trajectories can be influenced by the type and level of impairment that the care recipient exhibits, the relative stability of functioning level, and the physical and social environment of the caregiving context. As a result, knowing that a caregiving relationship has existed for 12 months does not provide a great deal of useful information about the specific needs of the caregiver, the caregiver's level of distress, or the prospects for continued caregiving in the future. There is a clear need for identifying critical markers of the caregiver career that are not necessarily directly correlated with the passage of time.

The analysis of growth, maturation, and change has frequently led to the search for markers of change that serve as alternatives to simple measures of duration or time. For example, the search for biomarkers of aging has highlighted the inadequacy of chronological age in explaining individual differences in longevity (see Arking, 1991). Similarly, in psychology, the notion of developmental stages has largely replaced chronological age in explaining individual differences in such diverse phenomena as intellectual development (Piaget, 1962), personality formation (Erickson, 1950), and moral reasoning (Kohlberg, 1963). So too, in caregiving, it makes sense to compare caregivers who are in like circumstances or similar stages of the caregiving process. Doing so, however, requires the identification of "markers" or features of the caregiving process that character-ize particular stages of the caregiving process in terms of "caregiving time" rather than real time.

The conceptual framework advanced here consists of the identifi-cation of seven major markers of caregiving careers which can be viewed as outcomes or consequences of other causal processes. That is, the factors that determine the caregiving experience are likely to be different at different points in the caregiving career. Thus, the experiences of caregivers at different career stages are hypothesized to be different as well. Although one could conceivably attempt to identify and measure all of the factors impinging on a caregiver at a particular point in time and use these factors to create some form of algorithm to assess need for treatment, several problems militate against such an approach. First, many of these factors have yet to be identified. Second, these factors almost certainly change over time. And third, any realistic model of need would almost certainly be very complex and consequently not particularly useful as a guide for implementing interventions in applied settings. A more effective approach is to use a model of need that incorporates these factors but does not require their direct assessment.

Career Markers

The first marker is reached when (1) a caregiver first performs caregiving tasks. The subsequent markers are (2) self-definition as a caregiver, (3) provision of personal care, (4) seeking out or using assistive services, (5) consideration of institutionalization, and (6) actual nursing home placement, and (7) termination of the care-giving role. Not every caregiver is presumed to reach each successive stage or to experience the event or status captured by each marker. The markers are presumed to be ordinal in their timing. The order of the markers, however, and the latency between markers are hy-pothesized to be variable depending upon both structural and indi-vidual circumstances. Indeed, the order of markers 2 through 5 and the differences in the time lag between these markers are viewed as important defining characteristics of the caregiver experience.

Marker 1: Performing Caregiving Tasks.   The first proposed marker of the caregiving career is the emergence of a dependency situation in which a family member or close acquaintance performs tasks designed to assist an older individual with routine activities previously performed without assistance. Two points are especially noteworthy. First, past research has generally failed to represent caregivers who are at this early stage. Commonly used "samples of convenience" generally recruit persons who define themselves as caregivers. We argue that self-definition is a later stage. Second, a basic assumption of our approach is that the informal caregiver role emerges out of another familial role or other pre-existing dyadic relationship (e.g., the roles of spouse, son, daughter, etc.). As a result, the form of the caregiving career (i.e., its duration and the tasks and responsibilities that characterize it) for caregivers whose roles have emerged from different familial roles (i.e., spousal vs. child-parent) and different norms of role enactment are inherently different. Our recent longitudinal research has demonstrated the differing temporal trajectories of caregivers depending upon their relationship to the elder (e.g., Montgomery & Kosloski, 1994).

Marker 2: Self-Definition as a Caregiver. Marker 2 is reached when individuals come to view themselves as caregivers and incorporate this activity into their social or personal identity. The relationship between role performance and identity is complex and can be viewed from a number of theoretical perspectives (e.g., see Brissett & Edgley, 1990). Nonetheless, most concur that performance of relevant role activities is an important component of identity. An obvious consequence is that, in order to be a caregiver, an individual must be providing care to someone. Performing certain tasks, however, does not imply that individuals will define themselves as caregivers. A major factor in the timing of self-definition is the role relationship between caregiver and elder, which need not occur contemporaneously with care provision. Self-definition most likely emerges out of shifts in the nature of the role relationship. For example, self-definition is likely to occur sooner in the caregiving process for adult children caregivers because caregiving to a parent represents a dramatic role shift. This is especially true if the care recipient changes residence to live with the care receiver.

In contrast, caregiving, at some level, is almost always part of the spousal role due to such factors as marital divisions of labor, power of status differentials, or individual differences in nurturance behavior. As a result, in the absence of a defining event (e.g., accident, heart attack, or stroke), the transition from spouse to caregiver may have an almost imperceptible onset and self-definition may be delayed. Self-identification as a caregiver by spouses may be particularly delayed when the primary reason for care is memory loss. Contrary to the situation experienced by adult children where the assumption of decision making responsibilities by caregivers is very apparent, the shift in decision making responsibility between spouses can be very gradual and experienced as part of normal everyday negotiations of spousal roles.

Marker 3: Performing Personal Care.   Marker 3 is reached when the caregiver begins providing personal care, such as assistance with bathing, dressing, bladder and bowel evacuation, or other aspects of personal hygiene. For caregivers who are children, this often represents an important decision point regarding whether to continue in the caregiving role; for spouses, it makes salient a further shift in the spousal role relationship from spouse to caregiver and may occur contemporaneously with marker 2. Since cultural norms define caregiving as primarily a female concern (Finch, 1990; Finley, 1989; Merrill, 1997), daughters are more likely to become care providers than sons. Moreover, there also appears to be a taboo against children providing personal care to their parents, especially sons providing care to mothers. The proscription of daughters providing care to fathers is substantially weaker (Montgomery & Kamo, 1989). Consequently, as the need for personal care increases for elders cared for by their children, the likelihood of terminating informal caregiving (e.g., institutionalization) increases substantially, especially for sons.

In contrast, whereas the need for personal care marks the end of informal caregiving for many children, it often signals an unambiguous start of caregiving for spouses. This delayed recognition of the caregiving role is especially likely when the care recipient has Alzheimer's disease and the provision of care to this point has involved tasks that could be viewed as spousal responsibilities. As a result, spouses are likely to reach markers 2 and 3 at approximately the same points in time and the order of the markers may be less consistent than for children. For these caregivers, the need for assistance with personal care is a graphic reminder that their relationship to the care recipient has changed in a significant way. It is an undeniable sign to the caregiver that the familial relationship that is most central to his or her life is fundamentally changed.

Marker 4: Seeking Assistance and Formal Service Use. Marker 4 is attained when the caregiver actively seeks or uses formal support services designed to assist informal caregivers. Such services include education programs, in-home respite, adult day care, counseling and support groups, chore or homemaker services, and home health care. A consistent observation of formal service providers and researchers has been that caregivers, especially spouses, have been shown to seek formal assistance relatively late in the caregiving career (Montgomery, 1991). Clearly, the decision to seek services is dependent upon factors other than the disability level of the care recipient. Whether or not a caregiver will choose to use an assistive service is dependent on at least three judgments: (1) that one's condition or situation is deficient in some way; (2) that a particular service will enhance or offset that deficiency; and (3) that the benefits of using a particular service outweigh the costs (both psychological and monetary) (Kosloski & Montgomery, 1994). Services for which the costs outweigh the benefits to users are unlikely to be perceived as useful. For example, if the wife of an impaired older person adheres to the belief that she is responsible for her husband's care, she may well experience serious guilt or embarrassment if she seeks the help of an outsider. On the other hand, as the wife's health deteriorates or as the burden of care increases, due to the increasing demands of caregiving or perceived loss of a significant relationship, the benefits associated with outside assistance will increase.

Understanding the determinants of marker 4 and differences among different types of caregivers in the timing of marker 4 may explain observed patterns of service use and failures of some intervention programs. Simply put, nonusers of services have not yet reached marker 4. That is, the experimental treatment being evaluated in these studies is not yet relevant to them. In contrast, participants who are at marker 4, or beyond, are using services, whether they are in "treatment" group or not. (Note: In the study of Lawton, Brody, & Saperstein 1989, use of nonexperimental respite by members of the "control" group actually increased over the course of the study.) The failure of these early demonstrations, from this framework, was in targeting appropriate study participants rather than in the failure of the services to perform their designed function. The present framework also explains why caregivers who use one service are likely to use other services as well (Hanley, Alecxih, Wiener, & Kennell, 1990; McFall & Miller, 1992).

The framework may also help explain differences in the patterns of service use that have been observed for adult-children and spouses. In particular, adult children tend to seek and use services earlier than do spouses and they have a greater propensity to use educational services. Since children reach marker 2 (i.e., self-identification as a caregiver) earlier in the caregiving process they are likely to reach marker 4 (seeking help) prior to reaching marker 3 (the provision of personal care). It is also possible that children caring for persons with Alzheimer's disease more readily view tasks that are related to memory loss such as making appointments or making decisions as caregiving tasks than do spouses and therefore tend to seek information about the memory loss and support services earlier in the disease process.

Marker 5: Consideration of Nursing Home Placement. The fifth marker is reached when the caregiver seriously considers placing the elder into a nursing home as an alternative to informal caregiving. The placement of this marker is not intended to suggest that caregivers never entertain thoughts of institutionalization until some point late in the caregiving career. Indeed, caregivers are first likely to consider institutionalization concurrently with self-identification as a caregiver. That is, self-identification results when the caregiver, having explicitly considered alternatives to caregiving (e.g., nursing home placement), rejects them in favor of the caregiving role. As changes in the caregiving situation occur, however, the caregiver may reconsider the earlier decision based on current circumstances. It is this reconsideration of placement in the context of terminating the caregiving role that characterizes marker 5.

Clearly, it is possible for caregivers to arrive at marker 5 without reaching marker 3 (performance of personal care) or marker 4 (use of services). This truncated trajectory, however, is most common for adult children. In contrast, many caregivers, especially spouses caring for persons with Alzheimer's disease, arrive at marker 5 simultaneously or very shortly after arriving at marker 4. These caregivers likely account for the "too little, too late" phenomenon that has been observed in respite demonstrations (Montgomery & Borgatta, 1989; Gwyther, 1989). When caregivers fail to seek services prior to seriously considering nursing home placement, there is little opportunity for services to play a preventive role.

Marker 6: Institutionalization. The sixth marker is reached when nursing home placement occurs. As many dependent elders die without ever residing in a nursing home, not all caregivers reach this marker. The lifetime risk of institutionalization in America is considerable, however, approaching 30% for all ages and increasing to over 45% by age 90 (Liang & Tu, 1986). Contrary to the preventive philosophy underlying support services for caregivers, past research has not supported the hypothesized negative relationship between use of formal services and institutionalization. Instead, formal service use has been found to be positively associated with institutionalization (Hanley et al., 1990; McCoy & Edwards, 1981; McFall & Miller, 1992; New York State, 1985; Pruchno, Michaels, & Potashnik, 1990).

Marker 7: Termination of the Caregiving Role. Marker 7, termination of the caregiving role, acknowledges that caregiving, like other social roles, can have an explicit end. There are three possible exit routes from the caregiving role: (1) death of the elder (or caregiver), (2) recovery of the elder, or (3) termination of the caregiving role (i.e., caregiver quits). The significance of this marker is that it acknowledges that care by informal caregivers continues to be provided after the elder has been institutionalized.

APPLYING THE FRAMEWORK TO UNDERSTANDING PATTERNS OF CAREGIVING

Variation in Caregiving Trajectories

The marker framework provides a tool for understanding variation in caregiving experiences and trajectories as well as a mechanism for understanding the conditions under which caregivers are likely to use support services. The greater propensity for spouses to provide more and more intense care than do adult children is not solely a consequence of different levels of felt obligation, but is also a consequence of different trajectories in caregiving careers. The careers of adult children and spouse are likely to differ both in terms of the factors that define the onset of the role and the factors that contribute to the abdication of the role. Many of the tasks that children consider a part of their caregiving role (e.g., assistance with transportation, banking, and household chores) are assumed by spouses as part of their marital role. Therefore, spouses tend not to recognize their caregiving role as separate from their spousal role until they begin providing personal care. For many spouses, then, caregiving can have an almost imperceptible onset, especially if the presenting problem is memory loss. In contrast, providing a parent with transportation, assistance with banking or shopping, or even decision making can represent a major role change for children. Consequently, children tend to identify themselves as caregivers at an earlier point in the caregiving process than do spouses and the point of transition to the caregiver role tends to be more easily recognized.

The earlier self-identification by children into the caregiving role has three consequences. First, children are likely to experience strain in their lives and to associate this strain with the caregiving role earlier in the care process. This experience of strain earlier in the elder's dependency cycle accounts for research findings that indicate children report a greater or equal sense of burden than do spouses although children are performing fewer care tasks (Montgomery & Borgatta, 1987; Johnson & Catalano, 1983; Young & Kahana, 1989). Second, adult children are likely to seek support services, especially educational services, earlier in the caregiving process because their earlier recognition of caregiving as a source of strain and because they have a lower level of perceived duty to perform care tasks. Findings recently reported by the authors (Kosloski & Montgomery, 1996) from a study of users and nonusers of respite services are consistent with this conclusion.

Third, children are more likely to leave the caregiving role when the impaired elder is at earlier stages in the disease and dependency process (Montgomery & Kosloski, 1994). For children, the structural conditions that keep the person in the caregiving role are decidedly weaker. Since there are no legal obligations and limited familial expectations for adult children to provide care, those children for whom caregiving would be an extremely difficult proposition are unlikely to assume the caregiving role in the first place. And when caregiving interferes with other familial and work obligations, there are generally fewer normative and psychological sanctions (e.g., guilt) for abdicating the role (Merrill, 1997; Miller & Montgomery, 1990; Montgomery & Borgatta, 1987).

These differences in caregiving patterns are illustrated by the work of Montgomery and Kosloski (1994), who reported that the decision to place a parent in a nursing home was associated with greater cognitive and physical impairment of the parent and greater objective burden. Notably, however, a sense of duty or obligation was not associated with placement but children reporting greater affection were less likely to place their parent in a nursing home.

Failing to recognize early care tasks as unique from the marital role, spouses are not likely to experience the caregiving role as burdensome or stressful until their afflicted mate is very dependent. Even then, their greater commitment appears to make them persist and endure in the caregiving role even if it involves extensive personal care (Doty, 1986; Kleban et al., 1989; Montgomery & Kosloski, 1994). This greater endurance is demonstrated by the findings of Montgomery and Kosloski (1994), which indicate that the level of functioning of the impaired elder and the level of objective burden of the spouse were not related to nursing home placement. However, spouses reporting a greater sense of obligation were less likely to place an elder. This pattern is consistent with the finding reported by Kosloski and Montgomery (1996) that persons reporting a higher level of perceived duty were less likely to use respite services. Also, the presence of cognitive impairment was associated with nursing home placement. It appears that when the elder becomes sufficiently impaired by dementia to substantially alter the basic marital relationship, spouses are more likely to seek support services and to abdicate their caregiving role.

In summary, the caregiving experience of adult children tends to differ from that of spouses in several important ways. First, children have greater volition in their choice of the caregiving role and their choice of leaving the role than do spouses, who express and demonstrate a greater obligation to this role (Stoller, 1992; Doty, 1986). Second, the caregiving role of children tends to be more circumscribed and occurs in the earliest phases of the elder's impairment. Children tend to concentrate their efforts on transportation, assistance with money matters and shopping, and some household chores. Spouses do not define themselves as caregivers until the elder has reached a level of impairment at which most children abdicate the caregiving role (Montgomery & Borgatta, 1989). Consequently, spouses provide more care of all types and are far more likely to be providing personal care and extensive household care. Third, when spouses assume the caregiving role, they tend to shoulder the majority of the care burden, while children, especially sons, tend to share the workload more equally with their siblings or spouses. Finally, spouses who must contend with a significant change in the relationship that is most central to their lives tend to find the role more emotionally stressful, while children report that the role impacts on their time, energy and other familial relationships (Montgomery & Kosloski, 1994; Stoller, 1992; Montgomery et al., 1993).

The Impact of Culture

The marker framework also provides a useful tool for identifying and interpreting cultural differences in the caregiving experience. Just as generation and gender influence caregiving careers by influencing when and how the caregiving role is assumed and performed, cultural expectations can influence caregiving patterns (Lawton, Rajagopal, Brody, & Kleban, 1992; Merrill & Dill, 1990). Certainly there is cultural variation in the norms that are attached to familial roles. The daughter role in Latino families can be very different from the daughter role in Asian or Caucasian families. Moreover, in many minority cultures the daughter or son role may differ depending upon the birth order of the individual. Hence, differences in cultural expectations for a particular family role are likely to translate to variations in caregiving trajectories.

These differences in cultural expectations, in combination with differences in family structure that are associated with minority groups, can account for cultural differences that have been observed in care patterns and use of support services. Because minority women have a greater probability of being single, the prevalence of daughters as the primary caregivers is considerably greater among Black and Hispanic populations than among Caucasian populations. The limited number of studies of these cultural groups suggests that adult children account for almost 75% of the caregivers versus the 40 to 60% that have been found in studies of white populations (Chatters, Taylor, & Neighbors, 1989; Hinrichsen & Ramirez, 1992; Wallace et al., 1992). Consequently, the daughters providing care for minority elders tend to provide more household and personal care than is true in white samples, and they tend to express a need for and use more in-home services and adult day care when it is available (Hinrichsen & Ramirez, 1992; Wallace, Snyder, Walker, & Ingram, 1992). At the same time, minority families tend to include a larger number of persons in the caregiving constellation, probably reflecting the greater equality in care sharing observed for adult children (Chatters et al., 1989; Hinrichsen & Ramirez, 1992; Wallace et al., 1992).

Implications for Service Use

The marker framework illustrates that a caregiver's willingness to use assistive services is associated with the point in the caregiver career at which the caregiver is located. For example, the low use rate of experimental services by participants in past respite demonstration programs becomes understandable within this framework. That is, individuals who have not yet reached marker 2 and consequently do not yet define themselves as caregivers will likely perceive information or programs directed toward "caregivers" as being largely irrelevant to them. In the same way, caregivers who do not yet see the benefit of educational or assistive programs to their particular circumstance will not utilize them fully. When individuals reach the point of full receptivity (i.e., marker 4), however, such programs can be expected to have their greatest impact. On the other hand, after that point (e.g., marker 5), the elder's need has increased, along with increased caregiving burden, due to the consistent decline associated with Alzheimer's disease and caregivers now consider relinquishing the caregiving role altogether.

In sum, the framework provides an efficient vehicle with which to target caregivers reliably for services that will likely be most effective for them.

TARGETING SERVICES

Differences in caregiving roles often translate to different needs for and willingness to use support services (Haley & Pardo, 1989; Knight et al., 1993; Lawton et al., 1989). The support services for caregivers that are most commonly available are educational programs, support groups, and respite services that include volunteer programs, adult day care centers, and in-home chore and personal care services. Despite considerable consensus about the value of such services for alleviating caregiver stress and burden, a consistent research finding and lament of providers has been that support services designed to alleviate caregiver burden and stress go unused, especially by spouses, who have been shown to seek formal assistance relatively late in the caregiving career (Horowitz, 1985; Montgomery & Kosloski, 1995). This lack of service use has been attributed to (1) lack of perceived need on the part of the caregiver (Caserta, Lund, Wright, & Redburn, 1987), (2) inappropriate targeting of services to caregiver's needs (Horowitz, 1985; Montgomery & Kosloski, 1995), and (3) barriers created by providers in the way in which services are offered (Caserta et al., 1987; Gwyther, 1989; Gwyther, Ballard, & Himan-Smith, 1990; Kosloski & Montgomery, 1993; Wallace, Campbell, & Lew-Ting, 1994). Simply put, caregivers will not use services for which they perceive no need or for which the monetary, emotional, or physical costs of using the service outweigh the perceived benefits.

Educational Programs

Clearly, for a caregiver to benefit from an educational program, the information provided must match the caregiver's current need for information. Since children who provide care identify themselves as caregivers far earlier in the care process, their needs for information are going to be quite different than those of spouses, who are unlikely to seek help for themselves until they are in later stages of the caregiving process. In the earliest phases of caregiving (i.e., the phase when children are mostly likely to seek help), caregivers are most likely to seek information about the disease process, the availability of community services, and legal and financial information. In the later phases of caregiving, the point at which spouses are more likely to self-identify as caregivers, there is a greater need for behavior management support, help with coping skills, and information about in-home support services. This variation in caregiver needs and caregiver trajectories likely explains the limited impact that "shotgun" approaches to information dissemination through group education, materials development and media have had (Toseland & Rossiter, 1989; Toseland et al., 1989, 1992). Such approaches tend to overwhelm families with information that may not be relevant to their immediate situation and, at the same time, fail to reach caregivers with critical information until it is too late (Montgomery & Borgatta, 1989; Pearlin, 1992; Toseland & Rossiter, 1989; Toseland, Rossiter, & Labrecque, 1989). Recent evidence suggests that caregivers are more receptive to educational programs and benefit from these programs when they are appropriately targeted to the different contexts and when information is dispensed throughout the caregiving experience (Gwyther, Gold, Hinman, Smith, & Poer, 1994; Mittelman et al., 1993; Toseland & Rossiter, 1989; Zarit & Toseland, 1989).

Support Groups

Educational programs are often linked with support groups for caregivers. In the past, caregivers have been shown to benefit from support groups through decreased stress and subjective burden and increased active coping strategies and knowledge of community resources (Haley, 1989; Toseland, Labrecque, Goebel, & Whitney, 1992; Toseland & Rossiter, 1989). Again, however, there is some evidence that spouses benefit from support groups in different ways than do adult children. In particular, support groups can help spouses cope with changes in their marital relationships, encouraging them seek outside help and set aside time for themselves. Children benefit from support groups by extending their support network and gaining better knowledge of community services. The different needs and concerns of the two groups again suggest the need for targeted programs. There is also some evidence that support groups are more difficult for spouses to attend due to lack of transportation, lack of respite, and greater dependence of the care receivers (Haley, 1989; Gonyea, 1989). Support groups have also been predominately attended by white and middle-class caregivers (Haley, 1989).

Respite

Perhaps the most controversial finding in the caregiver intervention literature has been the failure of respite to impact either caregiver burden or nursing home placement (Montgomery & Borgatta, 1989; Lawton et al., 1989; Montgomery & Kosloski, 1995). While this has prompted some observers to dismiss respite as a useful support, more recent research suggests that the original negative findings stemmed from lack of use of respite services by a substantial portion of the eligible caregivers in the samples (Kosloski & Montgomery, 1995). This failure to use services becomes understandable when differences in caregiving trajectories are acknowledged. In early phases of caregiving, respite is not really appropriate, since these caregivers tend not to be performing intense care tasks and, in the case of children, are often not living with the care receiver. Therefore, many children do not perceive a need for respite. At the same time spouses may not identify themselves as caregivers until the very late stages of their mate's dependency. Consequently spouses are likely to perceive information about respite programs directed toward "caregivers" as being largely irrelevant to them. Only when caregivers reach the point at which they are providing extensive care *and* have identified themselves as caregivers will they reach the point of full receptivity to respite programs. Respite programs can be expected to have their greatest impact at this point (Kosloski & Montgomery, 1995; Montgomery & Kosloski, 1995).

Frequently, however, caregivers have gone beyond the optimal point of receptivity when they seek respite. Often, when a spouse seeks assistance through formal providers, he or she may already be considering relinquishing the caregiving role because of the elder's consistent decline and increasing caregiver burden. This is the point at which respite programs become "too little too late" and fail to serve a preventive function (Montgomery & Kosloski, 1994; Montgomery & Borgatta, 1989).

Clearly the social context of caregiving dyads has significant impact on the caregiving experience and its consequences. In the future, providers will be far more effective in their support efforts if they acknowledge and target both the diversity and the consistencies that social contexts create. Factors that must be considered for targeting include the family relationship and cultural background of the caregiver and the point or marker at which a caregiver is located in the career process. Attention must also be given not only to the content of the support service or interventions but also the quantity or "dosage" of the intervention. Finally, in recognition of the changing nature of the caregiving career, interventions to support caregivers must be flexible enough to change over time and afford continuity of support.

CONCLUSION

In summary, caregiving is a normal process but not a singular one. The conceptual framework presented here is intended to provide an understanding of caregiving as an emergent relationship that differs by generation, gender, culture, and individual family histories. Consequently the caregiving experience can be characterized as both diverse and consistent. The consistent patterns of the caregiving career create diverse consequences or impacts of caregiving that translate into patterns of differential need for and willingness to use supportive caregiver interventions. At the same time, the dynamic nature of the caregiving role results in changes in these needs and service seeking behaviors over time.

When the patterns of diversity are identified, it becomes possible to mold and target interventions to the different types of caregiving relationships and the different stages in the caregiving career. Furthermore, the dynamic nature of the caregiving process should underscore the importance of providing the correct "dose" of support at the correct time in the caregiving career and the need for flexibility and continuity in support services.

It is our hope that this framework will be a useful guide for the development of interventions that can be molded to the diversity and consistency of caregivers and to guide the assessment of interventions. Certainly, much work remains to more clearly identify the markers and consistencies.

Finally, a note of caution. Although we sincerely hope that the framework presented here will be useful for practitioners and policymakers who are responsible for the creation of supportive interventions for caregivers, we would be concerned if caregiver interventions were to be viewed as the nation's panacea for long-term-care needs. It is important that both policy makers and practitioners recognize the limitations of family capabilities in meeting the ever growing challenge of long-term care. While the creation of interventions to meet the mosaic of caregiver needs is laudable and desirable, we as a society are still faced with two critical questions. The first challenge was identified many years ago by Sommers and Shields (1987) in their seminal book on caregiving: "What is the best way that we can all care for our nations's older disabled citizens?" (p. 184). The second question is a corollary to the first, which has emerged out of recognition that women, especially low income and minority women, disproportionately carry the burden of long term care: among whom should the costs of long-term care be distributed? In our zeal to ease the load of caregivers, let us not become so focused on short-term solutions serving as Band-Aids that we fail to search for a more humane, satisfying, and egalitarian solution to the long-term-care challenge. Caregiving as it is practiced today is a short-term individual solution to what is in reality a societal problem requiring long-term public resolution.

REFERENCES

Arking, R. (1991). *Biology of aging: Observations and principles.* Englewood Cliffs, NJ: Prentice-Hall.

Brissett, D., & Edgley, C. (1990). *Life as theater: A dramaturgical sourcebook.* New York: Aldine de Gruyter.

Brody, E. M. (1990). *Women in the middle: Their parent-child years.* New York: Springer.

Cantor, M. (1979). Neighbors and friends: An overlooked resource in the informal support system. *Research on Aging, 1,* 434–463.

Caserta, M. S., Lund, D. A., Wright, S. D., & Redburn, D. E. (1987). Caregivers to dementia patients: The utilization of community services. *The Gerontologist, 27,* 209–214.

Chatters, L. M., Taylor, R. J., & Neighbors, H. W. (1989). Size of informal helper network mobilized during a serious personal problem among black Americans. *Journal of Marriage and the Family, 51,* 667–676.

Cicirelli, V. G. (1992). Siblings as caregivers in middle and old age. In J. W. Dwyer and R. T. Coward (Eds.), *Gender, families, and elder care* (pp. 84–101). Newbury Park, CA: Sage Publications.

Coward, R. T., & Dwyer, J. W. (1990). The association of gender, sibling network composition, and patterns of parent care by adult children. *Research on Aging, 12,* 158–181.

Cox, H. (1996). *Later life: The realities of aging.* Upper Saddle River, NJ: Prentice Hall.

Doty, P. (1986). Family care of the elderly: The role of public policy. *The Milbank Quarterly, 64,* 34–75.

Erikson, E. (1950). *Childhood and society.* New York: W. W. Norton and Co.

Evans, D., Scherr, P., Cook, N., Albert, M., Funkenstein, H., Smith, L., Hebert, L., Wetle, T., Branch, L., Chown, M., Hennekens, C., & Taylor, J. (1990). Estimated prevelance of Alzheimer's disease in the United States. *The Milbank Quarterly, 68,* 267–289.

Finch, J. (1990). The politics of community care. In C. Ungerson (Ed.), *Gender and caring* (pp. 34–58). New York: Harvester Wheatsheaf.

Finley, N. (1989). Theories of family labor as applied to gender differences in caregiving for elderly parents. *Journal of Marriage and the Family, 51,* 79–86.

Gonyea, J. (1989). Alzheimer's disease support groups: An analysis of their structure, format, and perceived benefits. *Social Work in Health Care, 14,* 61–67.

Gwyther, L. P. (1989). Overcoming barriers: Home care for dementia patients. *Caring, 8,* 12–16.

Gwyther, L. P., Ballard, E., & Hinman-Smith, E. (1990). *Overcoming barriers to appropriate service use: Effective individualized strategies for Alzheimer's care.* Durham, NC: Duke Family Support Program.

Gwyther, L. P., Gold, D. T., Hinman-Smith, E. A., & Poer, C. M. (1994, November). A low-cost educational intervention for caregivers of memory-impaired older adults. Paper presented at Annual Scientific Meeting of the Gerontological Society of America, Atlanta, Georgia.

Haley, W. E. (1989). Group intervention for dementia family caregivers: A longitudinal perspective. *The Gerontologist, 29,* 478–480.

Haley, W. E., Brown, L., & Levine, E. G. (1987). Experimental evaluation of the effectiveness of group intervention for dementia caregivers. *The Gerontologist, 27,* 376–382.

Haley, W. E., & Pardo, K. M. (1989). Relationship of severity of dementia to caregiving stressors. *Psychology and Aging, 4,* 389–392.

Hanley, R. J., Alecxih, L. M. B., Wiener, J. M., & Kennell, D. L. (1990). Predicting elderly nursing home admissions: Results from the 1982–1984 National Long-Term Care Survey. *Research on Aging, 12,* 199–228.

Henig, R. (1996). More elderly people may develop Alzheimer's disease. In C. Cozic (Ed.), *An aging population: Opposing viewpoints.* San Diego, CA: Greeenhaven Press.

Hinrichsen, G. A., & Ramirez, M. (1992). Black and white dementia caregivers: A comparison of their adaptation, adjustment, and service utilization. *The Gerontologist, 32,* 375–390.

Horowitz, A. (1985). Family caregiving to the frail elderly. *Annual Review of Gerontology and Geriatrics* (pp. 194–246). New York: Springer.

Johnson, C. L., & Catalano, D. J. (1983). A longitudinal study of family supports to impaired elderly. *The Gerontologist, 23,* 612–618.

Kleban, M. H., Brody, E. M., Schoonover, C. B., & Hoffman, C. (1989). Family help to the elderly: Perceptions of sons-in-law regarding parent care. *Journal of Marriage and the Family, 51,* 303–312.

Knight, B. G., Lutzky, S. M., & Macofsky-Urban, F. (1993). A meta-analytic review of interventions for caregiver distress: Recommendations for future research. *The Gerontologist, 33,* 240–248.

Kohlberg, L. (1963). The development of children's orientations toward a moral order. I. Sequence in the development of moral thought. *Vita Humana, 6,* 11–33.

Kosloski, K. D., & Montgomery, R. J. V. (1993). Perceptions of respite service as predictors of utilization. *Research on Aging, 15,* 399–413.

Kosloski, K., & Montgomery, R. J. V. (1994). Service use by family caregivers of Alzheimer's patients. *Seminars in Speech and Language, 15,* 226–235.

Kosloski, K. D., & Montgomery, R. J. V. (1995). The impact of respite use on nursing home placement. *The Gerontologist, 35,* 67–74.

Kosloski, K., & Montgomery, R. J. V. (1996, November). Utilization of respite services: A comparison of users, seekers, and non-seekers. Paper presented at the 49th Annual Scientific Meeting of the Gerontological Society of America, Washington, DC.

Lawton, L., Silverstein, M., & Bengtson, V. L. (1994). Solidarity between generations in families. In V. L. Bengtson & R. A. Harootyan (Eds.), *Intergenerational linkages: Hidden connections in American society* (pp. 19–42). New York: Springer.

Lawton, M., Brody, E., & Saperstein, A. (1989). A controlled study of respite service for caregivers of Alzheimer's patients. *The Gerontologist, 29,* 8–16.

Lawton, M. P., Rajagopal, D., Brody, E., & Kleban, M. H. (1992). The dynamics of caregiving for a demented elder among black and white families. *Journal of Gerontology, 47,* S156–S164.

Lee, G. (1992). Gender, families and elder care. In J. W. Dwyer & R. T. Coward (Eds.), *Gender and family care of the elderly* (pp. 120–131). Newbury Park, CA: Sage Publications.

Liang, J., & Tu, E. (1986). Estimating lifetime risk of nursing home residency: A further note. *The Gerontologist, 26,* 560–563.

Matthews, S. H. (1995). Gender and the division of filial responsibility between lone sisters and their brothers. *The Journals of Gerontology: Social Sciences, 50B,* S312–S320.

Matthews, S. H., & Rosner, T. T. (1988). Shared filial responsibility: The family as the primary caregiver. *Journal of Marriage and the Family, 50,* 185–195.

McCoy, J. L., & Edwards, B. (1981). Contexual and sociodemographic antecedents of institutionalization among aged welfare recipients. *Medical Care, 19,* 907–921.

McFall, S., & Miller, B. (1992). Caregiver burden and nursing home admission of frail elderly persons. *Journal of Gerontology: Social Sciences, 47,* 73–79.

Merrill, D. (1996). Conflict and cooperation among adult siblings during the transition to role of filial caregiver. *Journal of Social & Personal Relationships, 13,* 399–413.

Merrill, D. (1997). *Caring for elderly parents: Juggling work, family, and caregiving in middle and working class families.* Westport, CT: Auburn House.

Merrill, D., & Dill, A. (1990). Ethnic differences in older mother-daughter co-residence. *Ethnic Groups, 8,* 201–213.

Miller, B., & Montomgery, A. (1990). Family caregivers and limitations in social activities. *Research on Aging, 12,* 72–93.

Mills, C. W. (1959). *The sociological imagination.* New York: Oxford University Press.

Mittelman, M. S., Ferris, S. H., Steinberg, G., Shulman, E., Mackell, J. A., Ambinder, A., & Cohen, J. (1993). An intervention that delays institutionalization of Alzheimer's Disease patients: Treatment of spouse-caregivers, *The Gerontologist, 33,* 730–740.

Montgomery, R. J. V. (1991). Examining respite: Its promise and limits. In M. Ory & A. Dunker (Eds.), *In home health and supportive services for older people* (pp. 75–96). Newbury Park, CA: Sage Publications, Inc.

Montgomery, R. J. V. (1992). Gender differences in patterns of child-parent caregiving relationships. In J. W. Dwyer & R. T. Coward (Eds.), *Gender and family care of the elderly* (pp. 65–101). Newbury Park, CA: Sage Publications.

Montgomery, R. J. V., & Borgatta, E. F. (1987). Values, costs and health care policy. In E. F. Borgatta & R. J. Montgomery (Eds.), *Critical issues in aging policy: Linking research and values* (pp. 236–252). Beverly Hills, CA: Sage Publications.

Montgomery, R. J. V., & Borgatta, E. F. (1989). The effects of alternative support strategies on family caregiving. *The Gerontologist, 29,* 457–464.

Montgomery, R. J. V., & Datwyler, M. M. (1990). Women and men in the caregiving role. *Generations,* (Summer), 34–38.

Montgomery, R. J. V., & Hatch, L. (1987). The feasibility of volunteers and families forming a partnership for caregiving. In T. Brubaker (Ed.), *Family and long-term care* (pp. 143–161). Beverly Hills, CA: Sage Publications.

Montgomery, R. J. V., & Kamo, Y. (1989). Parent care by sons and daughters. In J. A. Mancini (Ed.), *Aging parents and adult children* (pp. 213–230). Lexington, MA: Lexington Books.

Montgomery, R. J. V., & Kosloski, K. (1994). A longitudinal analysis of nursing home placement for dependent elders cared for by spouses vs adult children. *Journal of Gerontology: Social Sciences, 49,* S62–S74.

Montgomery, R. J. V., & Kosloski, K. D. (1995). Respite revisited: Re-assessing the impact. In P. Katz, R. Kane, & M. Mezey (Eds.), *Quality care in geriatric settings: Focus on ethnic issues* (pp. 47–67). New York: Springer Publishing Company.

Montgomery, R. J. V., Kosloski, K. D., & Datwyler, M. M. (1993). *Factors defining caregivers. Final Report to the National Institute on Aging.* (Grant No. R01-AG05702), Gerontology Center, University of Kansas, Lawrence, KS.

New York State Department of Social Services (1985). *Respite demonstration project: Final report.* Albany, NY.

Pearlin, L. I. (1992). The careers of caregivers. *The Gerontologist, 32,* 647.

Piaget, J. (1962). The stages of intellectual development of the child. *Bulletin of the Menninger Clinic, 26,* 120–145.

Pruchno, R., Michaels, J., & Potashnik, S. (1990). Predictors of institutionalization among Alzheimer disease victims with caregiving spouses. *Journal of Gerontology: Social Sciences, 45,* S259–S266.

Sommers, T., & Shields, L. (1987). *Women take care.* Gainesville, FL: Triad.

Spitze, G., & Logan, J. (1990). Sons, daughters, and intergenerational social support. *Journal of Marriage and the Family, 52,* 420–430.

Stern, S. (1996). Measuring child work and residence adjustments to parents' long-term care needs. *The Gerontologist, 36,* 76–87.

Stoller, E. P. (1992). Gender differences in the experiences of caregiving spouses. In J. W. Dwyer & R. T. Coward (Eds.), *Gender and family care of the elderly* (pp. 49–64). Newbury Park, CA: Sage Publications.

Stoller, E. P., Forster, L. E., & Duniho, T. S. (1992). Systems of parent care within sibling networks. *Research on Aging, 14,* 28–49.

Stone, R. (1991). Defining family caregivers of the elderly: Implications for research and public policy. *The Gerontologist, 31,* 616–626.

Stone, R., Cafferata, G., & Sangl, J. (1987). Caregivers of the frail elderly: A national profile. *The Gerontologist, 27,* 616–626.

Stueve, A., & O'Donnell, L. (1989). Interactions between women and their elderly parents: Constraints of daughters employment. *Research on Aging, 11,* 331–353.

Tennstedt, S., McKinlay, J., & Sullivan, L. M. (1989). Informal care for frail older persons: The role of secondary caregivers. *The Gerontologist, 29*, 677–683.

Toseland, R. W., Labrecque, M. S., Goebel, S. T., & Whitney, M. H. (1992). An evaluation of a group program for spouses of frail elderly veterans. *The Gerontologist, 32*, 382–390.

Toseland, R. W., & Rossiter, C. M. (1989). Group interventions to support family caregivers: A review and analysis. *The Gerontologist, 29*, 438–448.

Toseland, R. W., Rossiter, C., & Labrecque, M. S. (1989). The effectiveness of peer-led and professionally-led groups for caregivers. *The Gerontologist, 29*, 465–471.

Walker, A. J., & Pratt, C. C. (1991). Daughter's help to mothers: intergenerational aid versus caregiving. *Journal of Marriage and the Family, 53*, 3–12.

Wallace, S. P., Campbell, K., & Lew-Ting, C. Y. (1994). Structural barriers to the use of formal in-home services by elderly Latinos. *Journal of Gerontology: Social Sciences, 49*, S253–S263.

Wallace, S. P., Snyder, J. L., Walker, G. K., & Ingman, S. R. (1992). Racial differences among users of long-term care: The case of adult day care. *Research on Aging, 14*, 471–495.

Wright, F. (1983). Single careers: Employment, housework, and caring. In J. Finch & D. Groves (Eds.), *A labour of love: Women, working, and caring* (pp. 89–105). London: Routledge and Kegan Paul.

Young, R., & Kahana, E. (1989). Specifying caregiver outcomes: Gender and relationship aspects of caregiving strain. *The Gerontologist, 29*, 660–666.

Zarit, S. (1990). Interventions with frail elders and their families: Are they effective and why? In M. Stephens, J. Crowther, S. Hobfoll, & D. Tennenbaum (Eds.), *Stress and coping in later-life families.* New York: Hemisphere.

8

Afterword: Dementia Caregiving at the End of the Twentieth Century

Marcia G. Ory

The chapters in this volume are an excellent reflection of improvements in dementia care and research that have been achieved in the past decade. Going well beyond the usual recitation of burdens experienced, the chapters emphasize what is known about the daily lives and functioning of persons with dementia. Needed attention is paid to how clinical assessments and treatments can be appropriately standardized, and how interventions can be tailored to improve the quality of life of persons with dementia as well as to reduce often overwhelming caregiving burdens. While this volume focuses on dementia care, its impact is much broader, with clear implications for the provision of quality care for any cognitive or physical impairment. The old adage that "aging in place" environments were good for persons of all ages is applicable to the current concerns about improving care for persons with dementia. While such persons may be among the most vulnerable and undeniably experience some unique care needs, efforts to enhance quality of dementia care will result in the identification of quality care practices appropriate for all frail elderly persons.

RESEARCH EFFORTS AT THE NATIONAL
INSTITUTE ON AGING

These chapters represent specific research and practice efforts conducted by some of the leading dementia care researchers and practitioners. To provide a national context, research activities under way at the National Institute on Aging (NIA), the leading federal agency for research on dementia, are described briefly. Starting in the late 1980s with the establishment of the Coordinating Unit on Burdens of Care for Alzheimer's disease and related disorders, NIA, through its Behavioral and Social Research Program, began to give special emphasis to social and behavioral research on dementia care.

Research has increased dramatically around eight topics specifically targeted for increased attention. These are (1) the prevalence of dementia and estimates of the future availability of family and professional caregivers; (2) supportive environments and everyday functioning of persons with dementia; (3) effects of caregiver distress on caregiver's health and health behaviors; (4) social and behavioral interventions that enhance family caregivers' capacities to deal with burdens of care; (5) the impact of different health and social service arrangements on persons with dementia and their caregivers; (6) the economic costs of dementia under different caregiving arrangements and reimbursement policies; (7) methodological research to improve assessment of the quality of life in cognitively impaired persons; and (8) caregiving in special populations, such as racial and ethnic minorities.

In addition to individually funded grants, in the 1990s NIA supported two highly visible coordinated activities: (1) the *Special Care Unit (SCU)* initiative, a set of 10 collaborative projects that examined the nature and effectiveness of care in institutional settings, and (2) *Resources for Enhancing Alzheimer's Caregiver Health (REACH)*, a six-site collaborative effort to test the effectiveness of different home and community-based interventions for helping families provide care to loved ones with mild and moderate dementia.

Special Care Units

Information documenting the numbers and types of SCUs across the country is now available from the National Evaluation of Special

Care Units. A new national census of specialty care was initiated in 1996 to document changes in care within nursing home settings during the past 5 years. Analyses reveal a marked growth in the number of SCUs from the early 1990s, as well as their diversity and evolution. While SCU effects are not as great as expected, several studies have documented positive impacts on residents' behavior and social interactions. The dichotomous label of SCU/non-SCU has proved less meaningful than a careful examination of the consequences of different care parameters (e.g., special staffing, training, programming, or environmental modifications). Data from all 10 sites have now been transferred to the coordinating center, where metanalyses of the impact of different care parameters will be conducted using common core measures developed for such use. Emergent findings have been published in several specially edited journal issues, such as *Alzheimer's Disease and Associated Disorders: An International Journal* (1994, Supplement 1); *Journal of Gerontological Nursing* (January 1998:Volume 24), and *Research and Practice in Alzheimer's Disease* (by the European Commission, forthcoming in 2000, see especially the comprehensive review prepared by Grant and Ory). Moreover, a National Work Group on Research and Evaluation in Special Care Units (WRESCU) was established to serve as a forum for disseminating findings to policy makers and practitioners (see the WRESCU homepage at www.WRESCU-NAC.org).

Resources for Enhancing Alzheimer's Caregiver Health

Using a common core assessment battery, REACH is examining the effects of psychoeducational support groups, behavioral skills training programs, family-based systems interventions, environmental modifications, and technological computer-based information services in Caucasian, Hispanic, and African-American families in Alabama, California, Florida, Massachusetts, Pennsylvania, and Tennessee.

While still in the recruitment stage, REACH investigators synthesized the existing literature on dementia care (see *Intervention Approaches to Dementia Caregiving*, edited by Richard Schulz, Springer Publishing Company, forthcoming, 2000). Analyses of the 1996 National Caregiver Survey sponsored by the National Alliance on Caregiving and the AARP confirmed that caregivers rated dementia caregiving as significantly more stressful than other types of family care.

Substantial scientific activity has centered on developing a common metric for understanding the relative influence of different intervention strategies. Recruitment for the REACH interventions ended for five of the six sites in spring 1999, and baseline data became available shortly thereafter. Results of the effectiveness of the individual interventions and an assessment of the impact of different intervention components across the different interventions will not be available until early in the next century.

CAREGIVING THEMES

Despite the diversity of research topics and the ongoing nature of some of the key research activities, several themes and conclusions are emerging in dementia caregiving research. Observations on a few of these general themes are highlighted below:

The Caregiving Context and Assumed Impacts

Estimates of the magnitude of Alzheimer's caregiving and associated burdens are dependent upon caregiver characteristics, which often vary in different studies. The context of the caregiving situation is an important factor that cannot be neglected. For example, spouses provide more care but often report less burden than that reported by other family members. Caregivers who live with the person with dementia have different support needs from those who provide care at a distance. The effectiveness of interventions to reduce caregiver impacts can be affected by entry-level burdens reported: if caregiver burdens are too great, intervention efforts may be too late to make a difference; if reported burdens are too light, no intervention effects will be found. The influence of entry-level caregiver stresses, responsibilities, and burdens on study outcomes underlines the importance of appropriate targeting of the intervention to the caregiver situation and needs.

Designing and Tailoring Interventions

The research field is moving from broad evaluations of global intervention efforts to the design and assessment of particular interventions that are theory-based and generalizable. The success or failure of interventions is often difficult to interpret without attention to the specific intervention components that made a difference and to the mechanisms of action. The REACH project is providing an example of how different intervention efforts can be arrayed on a similar scale based on their primary goals. Researchers and practitioners need to specify their interventions carefully, examining the extent to which the proposed intervention efforts were actually delivered and received by the intended audience. The tailoring of interventions to individual needs can be accommodated within a rigorous evaluation process by carefully describing the processes and algorithms by which different intervention content is provided.

Identifying Mediating Factors and Care Outcomes

Intervention researchers are now required to make the linkages between intervention efforts and anticipated outcomes explicit. This involves identifying the role of mediating factors that can impact on desired outcomes, e.g., the nature of the caregiving burdens, the caregivers' personal beliefs, or the availability of other treatments or supports.

Equally important is attention to desired outcomes. Research has shown an interactive effect between caregiver and care receiver, suggesting the importance of measuring impacts for both. In the SCU project, the importance of measuring impacts on the nursing home resident, the family, the staff, and even cognitively intact residents residing in the same nursing home became obvious for understanding the complex interactive effects of different care patterns. For example, while integrated units may be beneficial for some demented residents, research generally shows that the cognitively intact are often happier in segregated units.

What are appropriate outcomes of concern? While economic outcomes cannot be ignored, behavioral and functional outcomes are also important and need rigorous study. The strength of collaborative studies such as the SCU initiative or REACH is the development of a common set of measures that can examine intervention effects across a wide variety of settings and populations. Recent work on measuring affect and quality of life in cognitively impaired people offers the promise of better assessment tools in these important areas. Additionally, greater attention is now being paid to biopsychological linkages between caregiving stressors and health outcomes with studies more carefully examining the physiological consequences of the caregiving role.

Transitions Across Care Needs and Caregiving Settings

While family caregivers still provide the majority of care, there is an emergence of new care options as care needs increase. Too often, caregiving issues are viewed statically. Attention to dynamic concepts (career or transitions) has become an important theme in caregiver research. It is critical to identify where caregivers are along the caregiver career: are they just starting out or have they been providing care for a long period of time? Some research efforts recognize the instability of new care situations and do not enter caregivers into studies at transition points. Other researchers or service delivery practitioners specifically target transitions as vulnerable periods needing focused research attention.

Another credible research strategy is to target the transition of service needs as a major outcome of interest. In this scenario, a major outcome would be to slow any declines in function or to postpone movement from the current setting of care to a more intense setting (e.g., from home to adult day care, to assisted living, to institutional care).

Diversity in Caregiving Situations

This past decade has been a time of learning about dementia and dementia caregiving in special populations. Despite some gains, most research is still conducted with middle-class white populations. Similarly, more is known about how women (as compared to men) manage caregiving responsibilities and burdens. There is now a concerted effort at NIA to encourage research on strategies for improving recruitment and retention of women and minorities in health and aging research, on developing culturally sensitive assessment tools, and on designing interventions that are appropriate to minority populations and settings. Recruitment and retention of special populations is more challenging, but studies such as REACH show it can be accomplished through extra attention and care.

SUMMARY

As illustrated in the chapters in this volume, our knowledge base about dementia care has grown dramatically over the past decade. Whereas dementia care was often a neglected area at the beginning of the decade, efforts in this area are now giving direction to more general long-term care research and practice issues. As we approach the next century, what will the future hold? Although the intensified efforts put into brain research and drug discoveries are promising a redefinition of dementia, it is likely, at least for the near future, that an increasing number of persons in our aging society will still be afflicted with dementia and its debilitating consequences. Attention to strategies for maximizing independent functioning and reducing dementia care burdens should remain a priority for researchers, service delivery professionals, and policymakers alike in the first decade of the new century.

Index